DREA
AND
INTERPRETATIONS

By
Allamah Muhammad Bin Sireen رحمة الله

English Rendering:
Moulana Muhammad Rafeeq Hathurani

Islamic Book Service (P) Ltd.

Dreams & Interpretations

By Allamah Muhammad Bin Sireen رحمة الله عليه

English Rendering:
Moulana Muhammad Rafeeq Hathurani

ISBN 81-7231-314-4

First Edition : 2000
Reprint   : 2012

Published by *Abdus Sami* for

Islamic Book Service (P) Ltd.

1511-12, Pataudi House, Darya Ganj,
New Delhi-110 002 (INDIA)
Tel.: 011-23244556, 23253514, 23269050, 23286551
FAX: 011-23247899, 23277913
e-mail: info@ibsbookstore.com
Website: www.ibsbookstore.com

Our Associates

♦ Azhar Academy Ltd., London (U.K.)
  Tel.: 020-8911-9797

♦ Lautan Lestari (Lestari Books), Jakarta (Indonesia)
  Tel.: 0062-21-35-23456

♦ Husami Book Depot, Hyderabad (India)
  Tel.: 040-6680-6285

Printed in India

CONTENTS

Section 1
INTRODUCTION: The Etiquettes of Interpreting Dreams

Dreams _ a Portion of Nabuwwah	1
Interpretation According to the Contrasting Meaning of Things	5
Interpretation According to the Varying Conditions in People	7
Interpretation According to Varying Times	7
Times in which Dreams are Most Potent	7
Facts to be Taken into Consideration Before a Mu'abbir Interprets a Dream	7

Section 2
Seeing Allah in the Dream

Standing Before Allah	10
Seeing Allah in Someone's House	10
Allah Warning Someone	10
Allah Occupying Someone's Bed	10
Seeing Allah in the Form of a Picture	10
An Incident	11

Section 3
Dreaming of Angels, Messengers, Saints, Ulama, the Ka'bah, Athaan, Salaah and Hajj

The Angels	12
Seeing Any of the Great Angels of Allah Ta'ala	12
Angels in the Masjid	12
An Unidentified Angel	12
Seeing Rasoolullah ﷺ in the Dream	12
Rasoolullah ﷺ in a Pleasant Mood	13
Rasoolullah ﷺ on Dry Land	13
When a Person in Grief Sees Rasoolullah ﷺ	13
Rasoolullah ﷺ in the Courtyard	13
A Most Unpleasant Dream	13
Rasoolullah ﷺ in Beautiful Garments	13
Seeing Rasoolullah ﷺ walking	13
Rasoolullah ﷺ Delivering a Khutbah	13
Rasoolullah ﷺ Looking into the Mirror	13
Rasoolullah ﷺ Eating Something	14

Rasoolullah ﷺ Presenting a Gift   14
The Ambiyaa ﷺ   14
Becoming a Nabi   14
Ulama and Saints   14
The Ka'bah   14
Seeing the Ka'bah in any Place Other than Makkah   14
Tawaaf of Ka'bah   14
Viewing the Ka'bah   14
Placing the Ka'bah Behind One's Back   15
An Incident   15
Performing Salaah in the Ka'bah   15
Inability to Determine the Qiblah   15
Making Additions to Salaah   15
Salaah Towards East or West   15
Embracing Judaism, Christianity or Fire-Worship   16
Idol Worship   16
Fire Worship   16
Imaamat   16
Athaan   16
Hearing the Athaan in any Month Other than Thil-Hijjah   17
An Incomplete Athaan during the Month of Hajj   17
An Incomplete Athaan during any Month Other than Hajj   17
Calling Out the Athaan in Strange Words   17
Broken Minaret   17
Erecting a Masjid   17
Sneezing   17
Shaving the Head   17
Khutbah   18
A True Story   18
Reciting the Holy Qur'aan   18

Section 4

Seeing the Skies, Sun, Moon, Stars, Planets, Qiyaamah, Jannah, Jahannam and Fire in One's Dream

Ascending the Sky or Heavens   19
Entering the Heavens without Ascending   19
The Sun   19
Holding the Sun   19
Solar Eclipse   19
Quarrelling or Disputing with the Sun   19
Sunrise in the House   20
Clouds Enshrouding the Sun   20

Narration   20
The Moon   20
Possessing the Moon   20
Lunar Eclipse   20
Moon in the Lap   20
The Moon in the House or Bed   21
The Moon of the First Night of the Lunar Month   21
The Stars and Planets   21
Possessing the Stars   21
Eating Stars   22
Collecting Stars   22
Stars on the Earth   22
Stars in the Hand   22
Falling Stars   22
Rotation of the Skies   22
The First Story   22
The Second Story   23
The Third Story   23
Day of Judgment or Qiyaamah   23
Standing before Allah   23
Jannah   24
Eating the Fruits of Jannah   24
Acquiring but Not Eating the Fruits of Jannah   24
Streams of Jannah   24
Garments of Jannah   24
Gardens, Rivers and Damsels of Jannah   24
Jahannam or Hell   24
Admission into Hell   24
Fire of the World   24
Fire Descending from the Skies   25
Fire Ascending the Skies   25
Basking before a Fire   25
Roasting Meat   25
Eating Roasted Meat   25
Cooking Food in a Pot   25
An Empty Pot on the Fire   26
Garments Burning   26
Eating Fire   26
Scorching by Fire   26
Branding with Fire   26
Sparks   26
A Burst of Flame in the Hand   26
Fire in the Market Place   26
A Burning Lamp   26

Light Given off by Fire   27
Collecting or Carrying Ashes   27
Collecting Fire that does not Burn   27

Section 5

Dreaming of Rain, Lightning, Thunder, Wells, the Ocean, Rivers, Canals, Vessels, Mills, Winds and Public Baths

Rain   28
Rain of Milk and Honey   28
True Stories   28
Thunder with Wind   29
Lightning   29
A Rainbow   29
Floods   29
Clouds   29
Possessing, Gathering or Walking in a Cloud   29
A True Story   29
Hail, Ice, Frost and Snow   30
Water Becoming Ice   30
Well   30
Digging a Well   30
A Well in the House   30
Irrigating One's Land   31
Wasting Water   31
Drawing Water from a Well   31
Watering a Tree   31
Giving People Water to Drink   31
Impurities in the Water   31
A Broken Bucket   31
Falling into the Well   31
Plunging into the River   31
Drinking Clean Water from the River   32
Drinking Unclean Water from the River   32
Bathing in the River   32
Crossing a River   32
The Sea or Ocean   32
Drinking Sea Water   32
Drowning   33
Walking on the Sea   33
Vessel or Ship   33
Boarding or Sitting in a Vessel   33
Water in the Vessel   33
Disembarking a Vessel   33

Vessel on Dry Land   33
Stream   34
A Stream in the House   34
Wudhu and Ghusl   34
Water in a Dish or Bowl   34
Drinking Water   35
Water in a Glass Tumbler   35
Wudhu and Ghusl with Milk, Wine, Oil etc.   35
Incomplete Wudhu   35
Complete Wudhu or Ghusl   35
Soil and Mud   35
Hot Water   35
Brick   36
A Brick Falling from a Wall   36
Bathroom   36
Urinating in a Bathroom   36
A General Rule Pertaining to a Dream with Two Scenes with
    Opposing Interpretations   36
Grinding Stones   36
Winds and Storms   37

Section 6

Seeing the Earth, Mountains, Deserts, Hills, Structures, Forts, Shops, Houses, Buildings, Explosions, Earthquakes etc. in One's Dream

The Earth   38
Standing in a Vast Stretch of Land   38
A Narrow Piece of Land   38
Dialogue with the Earth   38
Disappearance into the Earth   38
The Earth Revolving   39
Traversing through Wasteland, Wilderness or the Desert   39
Eating and Drinking in the Wild   39
Soil and Sand   39
Walking on Sand or Picking up Sand   39
Sand or Dust Flying in the Atmosphere or Skies   39
Digging the Earth   39
A True Incident   39
Mountains and Hills   40
Climbing a Mountain   40
Rocks and Stones   40
Pebbles   40
Standing on Top of a Mountain   40
Conquering or Dropping a Mountain   40

Digging a Hole in the Mountain   40
Ascending a Mountain without Faltering   40
Ascending   41
Carrying a Mountain   41
Shops and their Frontage   41
An Unknown House   41
A Known House   41
Possessing a House   41
An Extended House   41
A Ruined House   42
Selling a House   42
Building a House   42
Building a House in an Unknown Locality   42
Demolishing a House   42
Mansion   42
Wall   42
A Plastered or Cemented House   42
An Unplastered House   42
Climbing the Upper Portions of House   42
A Familiar House   43
Sweeping a House   43
Digging a Grave   43
A City in Ruins   43
Ladder or Stairs   43
Stairs of Unbaked Bricks   43
Stairs of Baked Bricks, Timber or Plastered Mortar   43
A Door   43
The Lintel   44
A Gutted House   44
A Displaced Door   44
A Dislodged Door or Doorframe   44
Someone Sitting on a Dislodged Door   44
A Door Falling   44
Doorframes   44
Closing the Door   44
Opening a Closed or Locked Door   44
A Nail   44
A Bridge   44
Earthquakes and Tremors   44

Section 7

Seeing Trees, Gardens, Orchards, Fruits, Vegetable, Crops etc. in the Dream

Trees   46

Timber and Firewood — 46
Twigs — 46
Staff (Asaa) — 46
A Thorn Tree — 46
Vineyard — 46
Pomegranate During its Season — 47
Eating a Sweet Pomegranate — 47
Sour Pomegranate — 47
Apples — 47
Oranges — 47
Yellow Fruit — 47
Green Fruit — 47
Watermelon — 47
Bananas — 47
Grapes — 48
Eating a Specific Number of Grapes — 48
Black Grapes — 48
Pressing Grapes — 48
Pressing Olives — 48
Olive Oil — 48
Black or Red Raisins — 48
Figs — 48
Walnuts — 48
Almonds and Pistachios — 48
Hazelnuts — 48
Non-fruit-bearing Trees — 48
Sweet-smelling Trees — 49
Odorous Trees — 49
Wheat — 49
Barley — 49
Flour — 49
Bread or Roti Made of Flour — 49
Dough — 49
Kneading Dough — 49
Rice — 49
Sesame — 49
Corn and Millet — 49
Beans — 50
Chickpeas (Chana), Lentils (Masoor) and Peas — 50
A Field Meant for Growing Produce — 50
Reaping a Field — 50
Sewing Seeds — 50
Seeds Grown into Plants or Trees — 50
Vegetable — 50

Sweet Smelling Flowers   50
Unknown Greenery   50
Dry Grass   51
Garden   51
Eating Fruits in the Garden   51
Pleasure in the Garden   51
Broken Gate of a Garden   51
An Unknown Garden   51

Section 8

Dreaming of Milk and Other Beverages

Milk   52
Drinking Fresh Milk   52
Drinking Curd or Whey   52
Cheese   52
Cow Milk, Camel Milk and Buffalo Milk   52
Milk of Wild Camel   52
Mule Milk   52
Donkey Milk   52
Milk of Game   52
Horse Milk   52
Lioness Milk   52
Milk of a Bitch   53
Vixen Milk   53
Sow's Milk   53
Drinking Milk from the Breast   53
Breast Filling with Milk   53
Wine   53
Intoxicants Made from Dates or Grapes   53
Intoxication   53
Drinking Wine   53
Brewing Wine   53
River of Wine   53
Honey   54

Section 9

Dreaming of Men, Women and Animals

Conversing   55
Seeing an Unknown Person   55
An Old Man   55
An Old Woman   55
A Young Girl   55
A Newborn Girl   55
A Newborn Boy   55

Eunuchs ... 56
Head ... 56
A Dismembered Head ... 56
The Hair of the Head ... 56
Shaving the Head ... 56
Long Hair ... 56
Dishevelled Hair ... 56
White Hair ... 56
Black Hair ... 57
The Face and Beard ... 57
A Long Beard ... 57
A Shaven Beard ... 57
Removing the Hair of the Head and the Beard Simultaneously ... 57
Dyeing the Hair of the Head ... 57
Rubbing Oil on the Hair, Beard or Body ... 57
Fragrant Oil ... 57
Smoke ... 57
Seeing Hair on the Palm ... 57
Hair of the Armpits, the Hair Below the Navel and the Moustache ... 58
Hair of the Human Body ... 58
Urine ... 58
Human Brain ... 58
Human Flesh ... 58
The Ear ... 58
Embellishment of the Ear ... 58
The Faculty of Hearing ... 58
Voice ... 58
The Eye ... 59
Applying *Kuhl* or *Surma* to the Eye ... 59
Eyebrows and Eyelashes ... 59
The Nose and Forehead ... 59
The Temples, Cheeks and Jaws ... 59
The Lips ... 59
The Tongue ... 59
The Front Two Teeth—Upper and Lower ... 60
Loose Teeth ... 60
Teeth in the Pocket ... 60
Masticating Teeth ... 60
Long Teeth ... 60
Molars ... 60
Canine ... 60
Pre-molars ... 60
Molars and Pre-molars ... 60
An Incident ... 61

Neck   61
The Brain   61
The Hand and Arms   61
An Amputated Hand   61
A Detached Hand with no Bleeding   61
The Hand Amputated by the King   62
Long Arm   62
Powerful Hands   62
Fingers   62
Nails   62
Bosom   62
Breasts   62
Stomach   62
The Stomach, Intestines and Other Organs   62
Eating One's Intestines, Liver and Kidney   62
Parasites   63
The Ribs   63
The Back and Loins   63
The Shoulder   63
The Male Generative Organ   63
The Testicles   63
The Left Testicle   63
The Thighs   63
The Knee   63
The Toes   63
Tendons and Muscles   63
The Skin   63
The Portions Between the Navel and Knees   64
Nakedness   64
Nudity in the Masjid   64
The Neck   64
Bleeding   64
Slaughtering a Man   64
Slaughtering a Haraam Animal   64
Killing a Person   65
Wrestling with a Person   65
Abusive Language   65
An Incident   65
Bridegroom   65
Divorce   66
Blood, Pus etc. without any Wound   66
Wounds, Bruises etc.   66
Leprosy   66
Insanity   66

Intoxication   66
Emaciation and Weakness   66
Power   66
Carrying a Burden   66
Excreta of Man and Animals   67
Droppings of Animals that are not Eaten   67
Becoming Spattered with Excreta   67
Passing of Stools   67
Passing of Anything besides Stools   67
Breaking Wind   67
Bleeding from the Anus   67
Spitting   67
Coughing   67
Blowing the Nose   67
Vomiting   68
Cupping   68
Cupping on the Neck   68
Bleeding from the Nose   68
Drawing Blood from the Vein   68
Blood in a Cup, Bowl or Tray   68
To be Stained with Blood, Dung etc.   68
Incidents Relating to this Section   68

Section 10

Dreaming of Weddings, Female Generative Organs, Pregnancy, Deliveries, Breast-feeding etc.

Wedding   71
Marrying a Dead Woman   71
Seminal Discharge   71
Greeting with *Salaam*   71
Marriage of a Wife   71
Marriage to One's Mother, Sister etc.   71
Marriage of a Man to a Man   72
A Woman with Male Generative Organ   72
A Woman with a Beard   72
A Man with a Pudenda   72
Menstruation   72
State of Impurity   72
A True Incident   73
Pregnancy   73
Delivering a Female Issue   73
Delivering a Male Issue   74
Delivery by an Expectant Wife   74
Breast Feeding   74

Section 11

Dreaming of Death, Dead Persons and Reports given by them

Death	75
Alive in the Grave	75
Digging One's Own Grave	75
Speaking to the Dead	75
Seeing a Deceased Person as Happy	76
Seeing a Deceased Person as Unhappy	76
Dying for the Second Time	76
Digging the Grave of a Dead Person	76
An Incident	76
Accepting from or Giving to the Deceased Something	76
Carrying the Dead	77
Embracing a Dead Person	77
Entering an Unknown House with the Dead	77
A Dead Person Entering the Home of a Sick Person	77
Giving the Dead *Roti*, Bread or Ring	77

Section 12

Seeing Clothes, Garments, Carpets etc. in One's Dream

Garments of Silk, Raw Silk and Fine Silk	78
Woollen Clothes	78
Sheet Worn as a Garment	78
Shirt or *Kurtah*	78
Old Clothes	78
Soiled Clothes	78
Dirt and Filth	78
White and Clean Clothes	78
Clothes that are Joined	79
Patched Clothes	79
Embroidered Clothes	79
Turban	79
A Silk Turban	79
A Woollen or Cotton Turban	79
Headgear or *Topi*	79
A Long Coat such as an *Achkan* or *Jubbah*	79
A Long Coat with a Lining	79
A Pair of Shoes	80
A Shoe	80
Good Smelling Sock	80
Torn Stocks	80

Leather Socks or *Khuff*   80
Wearing Torn Garments   80
A Wife's Garments   80
Head-cloth or *Odhni*   80
A Spinning Wheel   81
A Woman Acquiring a Spinning Wheel   81
A Wife's Donning the Clothes of her Husband   81
A Wife's Wearing the Military Clothes of her Husband   81
Donning Feminine Clothes   81
Donning Clothes of Various Colours   81
Donning White Clothes   82
Donning Yellow Clothes   82
Donning Green Clothes   82
Donning Red Clothes   82
Donning Black Clothes   82
Black Colour   82
Carpet or Mat   82
A Thick and Wide Carpet   82
A Thick but Narrow Carpet   82
A Thin but Wide Carpet   82
A Thin, Old, Torn and Short Carpet   82
A Handkerchief   82
Curtains   83

Section 13

Dreaming of Jewellery, Gold, Silver, Coins etc.

Jewellery   84
Acquiring a Pearl   84
Acquiring an Emerald or Ruby   84
Wearing a Pearl Necklace   84
A Burdensome Necklace   84
Earrings   84
Pearls Emanating from the Mouth   84
Eating Pearls   85
Scattering Pearls on the Road or in the Market Place   85
A Silver or Gold Necklace Studded with Jewels   85
Shells   85
Jewellery   85
A Waist-band   85
A Broken Waist-band   85
Crown   86
A Crown Seen by a Woman   86
Pillory   86
A Ring   86

Acquiring a Ring   86
Snatching a Ring   86
Theft of a Ring   86
The Stone of a Ring   86
A Gold Ring   86
A Ring Made of Iron   87
A Yellow Ring or a Ring Made of Lead   87
Wearing a Ring, Necklace or Earrings   87
Wearing Bracelets   87
Ankle-rings   87
Bracelet for the Upper Arm   87
Jewellery Worn by Women   87
Gold Coins   87
A Single Gold Coin or Coins up to Four   87
A Gold Coin without any Imprint   88
Bars of Gold   88
Coins of Silver   88
Black Coins   88
Black Coins Contained in a Bag   88
Giving Someone Black Coins   88
A Single Coin   88
Coins Made from Copper, Bronze etc.   88
Bars of Silver   88
Silver from its Mine   88
Bars of Iron, Steel or Lead   88
Smelting Gold, Silver etc.   89

Section 14

Dreaming of Vessels, Vases, Utensils, Mirrors, Scissors etc.

Vessels   90
Mirror   90
Needle   90
Threading a Needle   90
Threading and Sewing with a Needle   91
Sewing with a Threaded Needle   91
Sewing the Clothes of One's Wife   91
Comb   91
Combing the Hair and Beard   91
Scissors   91
Scissors Descending from the Sky   91
Clipping Hair or Wool with a Scissors   91
Glass   91

An Incident   91

Section 15

Dreaming of Arms, Weapons etc.

Theft or Destruction of a weapon   93
A Sword or Bow or Spear in the Hand   93
Killing Some Using a Sword   93
Striking Someone with a Spear   93
Injuring Someone with a Spear   93
Club   93
Inflicting Injury   93
Cutting a Limb   94
Receiving an Unsheathed Sword   94
A Broken Sword in the Sheath   94
A Sword in a Broken Sheath   94
A Sword with a Broken Handle   94
A Sword with a Good or Defective Handle   94
The Broken Point of a Sword   94
Wielding an Unsheathed Sword   94
The Sword-belt Hanging from the Neck   95
A Painted Sword   95
A Blunt Sword   95
Spear   95
A True Story   95
A Bow and Arrow   96
A Bow in its Cover   96
A Broken Bow   96
Discarding a Bow   96
Shooting with a Firearm   96
Shooting an Arrow   96
Shaping an Arrow   96
Confiscating a Bow from Another   96
Armour, Helmet etc.   97
Shield   97
Whip   97

Section 16

Seeing Horses, Mares, Mules, Donkeys etc. in One's Dream

Horse   98
Mounting a Horse   98
Defective Saddle, Reins, Harness, Stirrup Etc.   98
A Horse Having a Long or Short Tail   98

Limbs of the Horse   98
A Fighting Horse   98
An Uncontrollable Horse   98
A Flying Horse   99
Horses Running through Cities   99
A spotted Horse   99
A Black Horse   99
A Reddish-blackish Horse   99
A Brown Horse   99
A White Horse   99
A Red Horse   99
A Horse with White Feet   99
Allowing Another Person to Ride with   99
A Mare   100
A Black Mare   100
A White Mare with Black Spots   100
A Green Mare   100
Theft of a Mare   100
Eating the Flesh of his Mare   100
An Unknown Horse   100
A Pack-horse   100
An Obedient Pack-horse   100
Mounting a Pack-horse   100
Mule   101
Mounting a Mule   101
Mounting a She-mule   101
Mules of Various Colours   101
Seeing a Female Mule   101
The Skin and Flesh of a Mule   101
The Milk of a Female Mule   101
An Ass   101
Mounting an Ass   102
A Black Ass   102
Donkeys of Various Colours   102
Falling from an Ass   102
Dismounting an Ass   102
Buying an Ass   102
An Ass with Weak Eyesight   102
A Disabled Ass   102
An Ass Becoming a Mule   102
An Ass Becoming a Horse   103
A Weak Donkey   103
Eating the flesh of an Ass   103

Drinking the Milk of a She-ass 103

Section 17

Dreaming of Camels, Cows, Goats, Sheep, Their Meats and Colours

Camel 104
A She-camel 104
Riding a Camel 104
Fighting a Camel 104
Driving a Herd of Camels 104
An Unfamiliar Camel 104
Camel Meat 104
Eating Camel Meat 104
Milking a She-camel 105
Drinking Camel Milk 105
A Camel Calf that is Weaned 105
A Camel that has Escaped 105
An Ox or Bull with Horns 105
An Ox or Bull without Horns 105
Mounting an Ox or Bull 105
An Ox in the House 105
Owning Many Oxen 105
Being Hit with the Horns of an Ox 105
The Horns of an Ox 106
A Woman Mounting an Ox 106
The Flesh of an Ox 106
Slaughtering an Ox and Distributing its Meat 106
A Calf 106
A Herd of Oxen 106
A Cow 106
A Black Cow 106
A Herd of Black Cows 106
Lean Cows 106
A Fat Cow 106
Beef 106
Ghee and Milk 107
Milking a Cow and Drinking its Milk 107
A Pregnant Cow 107
Sheep 107
Acquiring a Sheep 107
Slaughtering a Sheep 107
Skinning a Sheep 107

Eating Mutton   108
Mounting a Sheep   108
Carrying a Sheep on the Back   108
A Sheep Mounting a Man   108
Overpowering a Sheep   108
Becoming the Owner of a Flock of Sheep   108
Sacrificing a Sheep   108
Ewe   108
Acquiring an Ewe   108
Slaughtering an Ewe for its Meat   108
Slaughtering an Ewe not for its Meat   108
The Ewe Escaping   109
All Products of Sheep   109
A Lamb   109
Receiving a Lamb as a Gift   109
Slaughtering a Lamb not for its Meat   109
Eating the Meat of a Lamb   109
Eating Half-cooked Meat of a Goat   109
Eating the Raw Meat of a Goat   109
Eating Roasted Meat   109
A Slaughtered and Skinned Goat Entering the House   109
A Limb of the Goat Skinned   109
Eating a Goat or its Limb   109
Eating the Flank or Ribs of a Goat   109
Becoming a Shepherd   110
Goat Hair   110
An Unknown Butcher   110
Buying Meat from the Butcher   110
Becoming a Goat   110
The Liver, Fat, Spleen etc. of a Goat   110
Eating the Innards of the Goat   110
Eating the Head of an Animal   110

Section 18

Dreaming of Game and Other Wild Animals, Their Meat and Milk

Wild Animals   111
Mounting a Zebra   111
Hunting a Wild Animals   111
Hunting Wild Animals that are Females   111
Hunting a Female Gazelle or Buck   111
A Wild Cow   111

Killing a Wild Animal with no Purpose of Hunting   111
Rabbit   111
The Young of Edible Game   112
Becoming the Owner of Wild Animals   112
The Skin etc. of Game   112

Section 19

Seeing Elephants and Beasts of Prey in the Dream

Mounting an Elephant   113
Eating Elephant Meat   113
Riding an Elephant in Battle   113
A True incident   113
Lion   115
Riding a Lion   115
Facing a Lion   115
Eating Lion Meat   115
The Skin of the Lion   115
A She-lion   115
Drinking the Milk of a Lioness   115
Tiger   115
Riding a Tiger   116
Drinking Tiger Milk   116
The Meat, Skin and Limbs of a Tiger   116
Panther   116
Drinking the Milk of a Panther   116
Hyena   116
Drinking Hyena Milk   116
Wolf   116
Drinking Wolf Milk   116
Cat   116
A Cat Entering a House   116
Killing a Cat   116
A Cat Fighting Someone   116
Mongoose, Lynx or Weasel   117
An Ape or Monkey   117
A Swine   117
Acquiring any Portion of a Swine   117
Drinking the Milk of a Sow   117
A Dog   117
A Barking Dog   117
A Dog that Attacks   117
A Dog Ripping the Clothes   117
Eating Dog Meat   117

Training or Holding a Dog   118
The Milk of a Bitch   118
Animals with Fangs   118

Section 20

Dreaming of Snakes, Scorpions and Other Creatures of the Earth

Snakes   119
Fighting a Snake   119
Being Bitten by a Snake   119
Killing a Snake   119
A Snake with Hands and Feet   119
Fearing a Snake   119
A Snake in the House   119
A Snake Leaving a Person's Ear or Stomach   119
Possessing a Snake   120
Possessing a Black Snake   120
Possessing a Beautiful White Snake   120
Possessing a Smooth and Beautiful Snake   120
Scorpion   120
Getting Stung by a Scorpion   120
Killing a Scorpion   120
A Scorpion in the Hand   120
Eating the Meat of a Scorpion   120
A Scorpion in the Stomach   120
Wasp   120
Ants   121
Mosquitoes and Butterflies   121
Bugs   121
Bugs Leaving their Nests   121
Locusts   121
Black Beetles, Dung-flies and all other Types of Files   121
Spiders   121
A Story Teller   121
A Mouse   121
Killing a Mouse   121
Incidents Pertaining to this Section   121

Section 21

Dreaming of Fish and Other Marine Creatures

Fresh Fish   123
Fillets of Fresh Fish   123

Salted Fish	123
Crocodile	123
The Flesh, Skin and Bones of Crocodile	123
A Frog	123
Frogs	123
Tortoise or Turtle	123
Eating Turtle Meat	124
A Turtle Walking on the Road	124
A Turtle in a Protected Environment	124
Crab	124

Section 22
Seeing Ordinary Birds, Birds of Prey and Poultry in the Dream

Birds of Prey	125
Acquiring or Owning a Vulture	125
Flying On the Back of a Vulture	125
Falcon	125
Kite or Eagle	125
Owl	126
Crow	126
Wood-pigeon	126
Crane	126
A Female Ostrich	126
A Male Ostrich	126
A Cock	126
A Hen	126
A Partridge or Pheasant	126
A Turtle Dove	126
A Parrot	126
Peacock	126
Peahen	127
A Honey Bee	127
A Ring-dove	127
Eating or Owning a Ring-dove	127
Acquiring the Feathers or Eggs of a Ring-dove	127
Hunting a Ring-dove	127
Nightingale	127
A Crested Bird	127
Sparrow	127
Hunting Sparrows	127
The Chirping of Birds	127

A Flock of Small Birds (Ababeel)   127
Starling   127
Raven   127
Marine Birds   128
Birds of Unknown Species   128
Eggs of Unknown Birds   128
Eating the Eggs of Unknown Birds   128
Eating Uncooked Eggs   128
Eating the Shell or White of the Egg   128
Incidents Relating to this Section   128

Section 23

Dreaming of Professionals, Manufacturers, Tradesmen, Entertainers etc.

A Person who Weighs and Measures   131
An Unknown *Qaadhi* or Judge   131
A Khateeb   131
Perfumer   131
Money-changer   131
Cloth Merchant   131
Treasurer   131
Tailor   131
Dealer in Hide and Skin   131
One who Mends Patches   132
Cobbler   132
Slave Trader   132
Carpenter   132
Blacksmith   132
A Wine Merchant   132
Launderer   132
Chef of Cook   132
Butcher   132
Sailor or Navigator   132
Goldsmith   132
Phlebotomist   132
Writer   132
Cotton-carder   132
Miller   133
Cup-bearer   133
Saddler   133
Dyer   133
Greengrocer   133

Minter 133
Barber 133
Shield Maker 133
Basket Maker 133
Teacher, Ustaad, Tutor etc. 133
Weaver 133
Treasure Collector 133
Builder 134
Surgeon 134
Astrologer, Soothsayer, Magician etc. 134
One who Makes Ta'weez 134
Conjurer or *Raaqi* 134
Fishmonger 134
Painter 134
Shroud-thief 134
Grave Digger and Excavator 134

Section 24

Miscellaneous

Noor and Darkness 135
Ruins and Desolate Land 135
Fort 135
Books and Magazines 135
Seal 135
Sealed Books 135
Books of *Fiqh* 135
The Holy Qur'aan 135
Desecrating the Holy Qur'aan 135
Limbs of the Body becoming Iron 135
Becoming a Slave or Prisoner 136
Limbs of the Body becoming Glass 136
Lending or Borrowing Something 136
Buying or Selling a Slave 136
Musk 136
Oud 136
Saffron 136
Usfar 136
Frankincense 136
Honey 136
Preparing Sweetmeats 136
Marriage 136
Sugar 137
Medicines 137

Eid   137
Mourning   137
Merry Making   137
Restriction   137
In Chains   137
Saddling a Horse   137
Chess   137
Dice   137
Chessman   137
Ink Pot or Ink Bottle   137
Pen, Pencil etc.   138
Desires Fulfilled   138

Section 25

Reciting the Various *Suwar* of The Holy Qur'aan in the Dream

Soorah Faatihah   139
Soorah Baqarah   139
Soorah Aale Imraan   139
Soorah Maa'idah   139
Soorah An'aam   139
Soorah A'raaf   140
Soorah Anfaal   140
Soorah Taubah   140
Soorah Yoonus   140
Soorah Hood   140
Soorah Yoosuf   140
Soorah Ra'ad   140
Soorah Ibraheem   140
Soorah Hijr   140
Soorah Nahl   140
Soorah Bani Isra'eel   140
Soorah Kahf   141
Soorah Maryam   141
Soorah Taha   141
Soorah Ambiya   141
Soorah Hajj   141
Soorah Mu'minoon   141
Soorah Noor   141
Soorah Furqaan   141
Soorah Shu'ara   141
Soorah Naml   141
Soorah Qasas   141

Soorah Ankaboot 142
Soorah Room 142
Soorah Luqmaan 142
Soorah Sajdah 142
Soorah Ahzaab 142
Soorah Sabaa 142
Soorah Faatir 142
Soorah Yaseen 142
Soorah Saaffaat 142
Soorah Saad 142
Soorah Zumar 142
Soorah Mu'min or Ghaafir 142
Soorah Ha-Meem As-Sajdah 142
Soorah Shoora 142
Soorah Zukhruf 142
Soorah Dukhaan 143
Soorah Jaathiya 143
Soorah Ahqaaf 143
Soorah Muhammad or Qitaal 143
Soorah Fat-h 143
Soorah Hujuraat 143
Soorah Qaaf 143
Soorah Thaariyaat 143
Soorah Toor 143
Soorah Najm 143
Soorah Qamar 143
Soorah Rahmaan 143
Soorah Waaqi'ah 144
Soorah Maa'idah 144
Soorah Hadeed 144
Soorah Mujaadalah 144
Soorah Hashr 144
Soorah Mumtahinah 144
Soorah Saff 144
Soorah Jumu'ah 144
Soorah Munafiqoon 144
Soorah Taghaabun 144
Soorah Talaaq 144
Soorah Tahreem 144
Soorah Mulk 144
Soorah Noor or Qalam 144
Soorah Haaqqah 144
Soorah Ma'aarij 144
Soorah Nooh 145

Soorah Jinn   145
Soorah Muzzammil   145
Soorah Muddath-thir   145
Soorah Qiyaamah   145
Soorah Dahr or Insaan   145
Soorah Mursalaat   145
Soorah Naba'   145
Soorah Naazi'aat   145
Soorah Abasa   145
Soorah Takweer   145
Soorah Infitaar   145
Soorah Tatfeef   145
Soorah Inshiqaaq   145
Soorah Burooj   146
Soorah Taariq   146
Soorah A'la   146
Soorah Ghaashiyah   146
Soorah Fajr   146
Soorah Balad   146
Soorah Shams   146
Soorah Layl   146
Soorah Duhaa   146
Soorah Inshiraah   146
Soorah Teen   146
Soorah Alaq   146
Soorah Qadr   146
Soorah Bayyinah   146
Soorah Zilzaal   147
Soorah Aadiyaat   147
Soorah Qaari'ah   147
Soorah Takaathur or Maqaabir   147
Soorah Asr   147
Soorah Humazah   147
Soorah Feel   147
Soorah Quraish   147
Soorah Maa'oon   147
Soorah Kauthar   147
Soorah Kaafiroon   147
Soorah Nasr   147
Soorah Lahab or Masad   147
Soorah Ikhlaas   148
Soorah Falaq   148
Soorah Naas   148

Section 1:   **INTRODUCTION**

The Etiquettes of Interpreting Dreams

Dreams_ a Portion of Nabuwwah:

Rasoolullah 鹵 is reported to have said that *Ru'ya* or dreams are a portion from the forty portions of *nabuwwah*. That is why every person is not privileged to give the *ta'beer* or interpretation of dreams. Only a person who has the following qualifications is authorised to do so:

(1) He must have adequate knowledge of the Tafseer of the Qur'aan.

(2) He must be a Hafiz of the Ahadeeth of Rasoolullah 鹵.

(3) He must be well versed in the Arabic language.

(4) He must be familiar with the roots of words so that he knows where they are derived from.

(5) He must be familiar with the nature and status of people.

(6) He must be familiar with the basic principles of *ta'beer* or interpretation.

(7) He must possess a pure and clean soul.

(8) He must be a man with sound morality.

(9) He must be honest in speech and conduct.

Why all the above requisites? Because when giving the *ta'beer* of a dream, at times, the aspect of time has to be taken into account and at other times, the *ta'beer* is given directly from the Qur'aan or Hadeeth and again, at other times, the usage and phraseology is taken into account. Sometimes, instead of taking into

consideration the one the one who sees the dream, the *Mu'abbir*
(interpreter) will take into account someone who resembles him
(i.e. the observer of the dream) in personality or name.
Sometimes an interpretation is given by a name only or by the
meaning of a word only or by its contrasting meaning. Again, at
other times the root-meaning of a word is taken into account, or
the lesser or greater meaning of a word is taken into account.

Examples of *Ta'beer* from the Holy Qur'aan:

(1) Allah Ta'ala says in the Holy Qur'aan: *As if they (the damsels
     of Jannah) are concealed eggs.*

     In the above verse, since Allah Ta'ala has assimilated the
     women of Jannah to eggs, eggs seen in the dream could be
     interpreted by the *Mu'abbir* as women.

(2) And stones or rocks could be interpreted as the hardness of
     hearts in the view of the following verse of the Holy
     Qur'aan: *Then your hearts become hard, then they become like
     stones or even harder than stones.*

(3) And flesh could be interpreted as backbiting in the light of
     this verse: *What! will one of you like to eat the flesh of his dead
     brother? (No) you will detest to do so!*

     In the above verse Allah Ta'ala has referred to backbiting to
     be the same as eating the flesh of one's dead brother.

(4) And keys could be interpreted as treasures because Allah
     Ta'ala says: *And We gave him (Qaaroon) so much treasures that
     their keys were carried by a powerful group of men.*

     Logically, the above interpretation is very apt because one
     may reach one's treasure through the medium of keys only.

(5) Likewise, a boat or vessel may be interpreted as deliverance
     or safety from any calamity, for, Allah Ta'ala says in the
     Holy Qur'aan: *Then we saved him (Nooh) and the people of the
     boat.*

     And He also says: *Then we saved him and those with him in the
     boat.*

(6) Similarly, if someone dreams that a king has entered

someone's house or a certain town contrary to his (the king's) normal habit, then this could be interpreted as some calamity befalling that house or town; or the humiliation of the noble people of such a town. This interpretation is given in the light of the following aayah: *Surely, kings, when they enter a country, they despoil it and make the noblest of its people its meanest.*

(7) Similarly, garments could be interpreted as women in the view of this vers: *They (your wives) are your garments and you are their garments.*

Examples of *Ta'beer* from the Hadeeth:

(1) A crow many be interpreted as a shameless and corrupt person because Rasoolullah ﷺ named the crow as *faasiq*, meaning shameless, corrupt etc.

(2) A mouse could be interpreted as a shameless and licentious woman because Rasoolullah ﷺ has said that a mouse is corrupt and shameless.

In the above Hadeeth the word *faasiqah* is used which is normally used for describing a corrupt and licentious woman.

(3) And the rib would mean a woman in the light of this Hadeeth: "A woman is created from a crooked rib".

(4) A doorsill or threshold may be interpreted as a woman because it is narrated that Ibraheem ﷺ said to his son, Isma'eel ﷺ: "Change your doorsil", meaning "your wife". There are thus, countless examples of delivering interpretation in the light of the Ahadeeth.

Examples of *Ta'beer* According to General Usage of Language:

(1) If a person sees that his arm is long, it means that he will treat people with kindness and generosity because the Arabic expression *his arm is longer than yours* means that he is more generous than you.

(2) Carrying wood in the dream means tale-bearing and gossipping. In Arabic the expression *he carries or is carrying*

wood is used when one carries gossip from one person to another.

(3) To see oneself or someone else as sick is interpreted as "hypocrisy". In Arabic the expression *so-and-so is sick in his promise* is usded when someone does not fulfil his promise.

(4) Mucus in the dream symbolises a son because the expression *the mucus of the lion is* used when a son resembles his father.

(5) To see someone throwing a stone at another or shooting an arrow at another or aiming a weapon at him means that such a person is talking bad of he other person because in Arabic, the expression *so-and-so shot at another* is used when someone backbites about another or falsely accuses him.

(6) To see oneself or another washing the hands with soap may be interpreted as despair, despondency and loss of hope. The expression *I have washed my hands off you with ushnaan* is used when a person loses all hope of acquiring any good or benefit from another.

These are only a few examples to demonstrate that many an interpretation depends on daily usage of the Arabic Language, idioms, proverbs and expressions. There are countless examples of this.

Examples of Interpretation According to the Overt Meaning of Names:

If a person bearing a certain name is seen in the dream or such a name is heard in the dream then the interpretation will be given according to the meaning of the name. Examples follow:

Fadhl, Faadhil, Afdhal denote excellence, superiority, kindness, generousity, honour etc.

Rasheed, Raashid, Arshad denote treading the straight path, to be preserved from error, be well-guided, right conduct etc.

Saleem, Saalim, Aslam denote soundness, safety, healthy, be without blemish, to be good-natured etc.

Examples of Interpretation According to the Covert or Deeper Meaning of Words:

A flower in bloom such as a narcissus or rose denotes shortness of life or imminent death since flowers do not remain forever. They are normally short-lived. Hence, a similar interpretation will be given regarding the person who owns or possesses flowers or towards whom such flowers are associated. Such examples are many.

Interpretation According to the Contrasting Meaning of Things:

Seeing oneself as weeping will be interpreted as joy and happiness as long as such weeping is not done with sound, screaming or tearing one's collar to pieces as when mourning. On the contrary joy, happiness, merry-making, laughter, dancing etc. will be interpreted as grief and sorrow.

Similarly, if two persons are seen fighting in the dream then the one who loses the battle will be the one to gain victory.

Similarly, if a person sees himself being cupped it means he will be compelled to fulfil certain conditions in an agreement or contract. Or if a person sees himself being made to agree on certain conditions, it means he will get cupped. The reason being that in Arabic the word *shart* (condition) is sometimes used to mean "cupping★".

Entering the Grave:

If a person sees himself being admitted or lowered in the grave it means he will be imprisoned. Or if a person sees himself being imprisoned in a place which is unknown to him and the people of a such a place are also unknown to him, it means he will enter the grave.

Attack or Assault:

If a person sees an enemy attacking or assaulting a group of people, it means a calamity in the form of a storm or flood is imminent.

★ Cupping: The use of a cupping glass from which the air has been exhausted, to draw blood to the surface of the skin _ Collins.

A Swarm of Locusts:

A swarm of locusts in one's dream represents an army. And an army of soldiers represents a swarm of locusts which will cause havoc and destruction.

If a swarm of locusts is seen approaching or flying without buzzing it represents one's wealth which one had accumulated secretly. But if it is with a buzzing sound it means enmity and hatred.

Long Hair:

Hair is interpreted as wealth and beauty. But if such hair falls upon the face or tufts of hair is seen on the cheek it suggests grief and sorrow. According to some people it could suggest beautiful garments as well.

Hair which is intertwined or folded or wrapped suggests that ill will be spoken of the observer of such a dream and that he will not be able to defend himself.

Feathers and Wings:

If a person sees himself having feathers and two wings it suggests that he will acquire wealth and riches. If he sees himself flying it means he will undertake a journey.

Severed Hand

If a person sees his hand severed and while lifting such a hand, it remains attached to his body it means he will derive some benefit from his brother or son. But if the severed hand is completely detached it means he will suffer some loss caused by his brother or son.

Illness and Recovery:

If a sick person sees himself as having recovered or sees himself as healthy and then leaves his house after conversing (with someone) it means that he will recover. But it he does not speak to anyone it means he will die.

Cities, Towns and Villages:

Cities, Towns and villages imply that the observer of such a dream will encounter unchaste women if such places are not of multiple colours. And if they are black and white then it suggests day and night _ ie. the alternating of day and night and the passing of time.

Fish:

If a person sees a specific number of fish in his dream it suggests that he will come into contact with a woman or he will marry a woman. But if its number or quantity is unknown it means he will acquire wealth or booty.

Interpretation According to the Varying Conditions of People:

If a righteous and noble person sees himself as handcuffed or placed in a pillory★ it means he will remain safeguarded against mischief and wickedness. But if the observer of such a dream is wicked it suggests that he will commit excessive sins due to which he will be doomed to hell-fire. May Allah, through His infinite mercy, save us from hell-fire. Ameen.

Interpretation according to Varying Times:

If a person dreams during the night that he is mounted on an elephant it suggests that he will profit immensely from a certain affair or contract or task. But if such a dream is observed during the day it means he will divorce his wife.

Times in which Dreams are Most Potent:

It must be borne in mind that the most authentic dreams are the ones observed in the latter part of the night and during *Qayloolah* (sleeping at midday) and during the day. Dreams during the fruit-ripening season and fruit-selling season are also very potent. The most inopportune time wherein dreams hardly have any significant meaning is during the winter season and when rain is imminent.

Facts to be Taken into Consideration Before a *Mu'abbir* Interprets a Dream:

It is imperative that *mu'abbir* or interpreter understands fully

---

★ Pillory: a wooden board with holes for the head and hands in which petty offenders were formerly and exposed to public scorn.

and properly every detail of a dream seen by any person. He should be able to weigh it on the scale of the rules of interpretation. If the numerous facts emerging from a dream are such that they correspond with each other logically then such a dream will be deemed as a genuine and authentic dream. But if the facts emerging from such a dream are such that they do not correspond with each other then the interpreter should reflect on the apparent meaning of the words. Whichever meaning is nearest to the rules of interpretation, such a meaning should be adopted.

If a dream is of complicated nature so that it cannot be weighed on the scale of the rules of interpretation then such a dream will be deemed as meaningless.

If a certain dream causes the interpreter to become dubious then he should appeal to the conscience of the observer of such dream: If the dream concerns Salaah, he should question him about Salaah; if it concerns a journey he should question him about the journey; if it concerns marriage, he should question him about marriage. Thereafter, the *mu'abbir* will interpret to the best of his knowledge.

The interpreter should be extremely cautious when interpreting a dream: if the dream evidences obscenity and indecency he should either use pleasant words when interpreting it or simply avoid interpreting it.

It is necessary for a *mu'abbir* to establish the biological and logical classification of things and give its interpretation accordingly The biological and logical classification of things can be made as follows: (a) geneses (b) species (c) nature and characteristics.

Examples of Geneses of Things:
Trees, Voracious animals and birds. If these are seen in ones dream (individually or collectively) they may very likely mean men.

Examples of Species:
A specific tree like the date tree or a walnut tree. The date tree many be interpreted as an honourable Arab gentleman since

date trees are mainly indigenous to Arab Countries. A s for the walnut tree, it represent a non-Arab person since these trees do not grow in the land of the Arabs.

The same applies to birds. If a bird is huge it symbolises an Arab gentleman; a peacock represents a non-Arab gentleman.

Examples of the Nature and Characteristics of Things:

A date tree. This may be interpreted as total goodness and virtue since the date tree is regarded as a tree constituting total goodness as is known from the Hadeeth. On the other hand a walnut tree may be interpreted as a person which is deceptive as well as quarrelsome. Why? Because it is by nature very hard and its core cannot be attained until broken or split open.

The nature of birds is to fly. Therefore, the one towards whom a bird is associated may be said to be travelling very often and widely.

A peacock may be interpreted as a wealth non-Arab king who adopts much embellishments and who has many followers. The same applies to a royal white falcon or eagle. But if it is a crow or a magpie, it represents an evil person.

As shown in the above examples, the *Mu'abbir* should be able to draw analogies before interpreting a dream. If he does so, he will be rightly-guided, by the will of Allah.

And guidance is from Allah alone.

Section 2 :

Seeing Allah in the Dream

Standing Before Allah: If a person sees himself as a pious and chosen servant of Allah, standing before Allah, beholding Him, and He, in turn looking upon him with mercy and clemency then such a dream is regarded as very blessed dream. For it means that he will meet his Creator in the same manner on the Day of Qiyamah. This dream is also a glad tiding that his good actions in the world are accepted by Allah and he will attain Jannah.

A Material Gift from Allah: If a person sees Allah giving him something pertaining to the world, it means he will soon be afflicted with sickness. It may also mean that some hardship will befall him. As recompense, he shall receive great rewards from Allah which will earn him Jannah.

Seeing Allah in Someone's House: Seeing Allah present in a particular house suggests that the occupants of such a house sill be favoured with peace, happiness and assistance.

Allah Warning Someone: If someone sees Allah reprimanding, warning or prohibiting him from doing something it means that he is indulging in abominable actions. He should reform without delay.

Allah Occupying Someone's Bed: If someone sees Allah occupying his bed, Congratulating him, then this is a glad tiding that Allah will grant him piety and sainthood and that Allah's blessings will descend upon him. For, a dream such as this is not viewed but by pious and righteous persons.

Seeing Allah in the Form of a Picture: One who sees Allah in the form of a picture or he thinks he has seen Allah or someone resembling Allah it means that the observer of such a dream is a compulsive liar_levelling accusations against Allah and indulging in innovations (*bid'aat*). It is imperative that such a person hastens towards seeking Allah's forgiveness. The same applies to a person who sees Allah in the form of an idol or any such form as is contrary to His excellence and sublimity. For, Allah Ta'ala is free from all blemishes and weaknesses.

An Incident: It is related that a man came to Ja'far As-Saadiq and said: "I dreamt that Allah gave me a piece of iron and a sip of vinegar. What is the interpretation of this dream?"

The Imaam replied: "Iron depicts hardships, for Allah says in the Qur'aan: *And we have sent iron wherein is material for mighty war.* But it is possible that your children may learn this trade of Dawood 🕮 (for he was a blacksmith by trade). As for vinegar, it means you will be afflicted with a disease for some time, at the same time acquiring abundant wealth. Thereafter, if Allah gives you death, he will be pleased with you and forgive all your sins, past and future.

❁❁❁

Section 3 :

Dreaming of the Angels, Messengers, Saints, Ulama, The Ka'bah, Athaan, Salaah and Hajj

The Angels: Seeing and angel in one's dream is a very blessed dream. The observer of the dream will attain honour and piety. The people of that town in which such a dream was seen will receive peace and assistance.

Seeing Any of the Great Angels of Allah Ta'ala: Dreaming of any of the great angels of Allah (such as Jibreel, Mikaail, Izrail and Israfeel 🕊️) heralds plentiful rain, fertility of land, abundant *rizq* and reduction in prices of goods or commodities. It is also a glad tiding that the observer of such a dream will attain martyrdom.

Angels in the Masjid: If angels are seen in mosques it means that due to the religious shortcoming of the people of that town, the angels are commanding them to engage in dua, salaah, charity and sincere repentance. If angels are seen in the market place it means they are prohibiting the people from dishonesty in measure and weight. And if angels are seen in the cemetery it means a great calamity will befall the pious servants of Allah.

An Unidentified Angel: If an unknown person is referred to as an angel in the dream then surely he is none other than a great angel of Allah Ta'ala.

Seeing Rasoolullah 🕊️ in the Dream: Rasoolullah 🕊️ has said: "Whosoever sees in his dream he has truly seen me. For, the devil is unable to assume my form".

Seeing Rasoolullah ﷺ **in a Pleasant Mood:** If someone sees the Holy Prophet ﷺ in a happy and pleasant mood then such a dream is in reality harbinger of goodness and happiness. And seeing him in an unpleasant mood will mean misery and hardship in the world for that person.

Rasoolullah ﷺ **on Dry Land:** If the Holy Prophet ﷺ is seen standing on dry, arid land, such land will soon become green and verdant (fertile)

When a person in Grief Sees Rasoolullah ﷺ**:** If a grief-striken, hard-pressed, poverty-stricken person sees Rasoolullah ﷺ in his dream then his afflictions and anxieties will soon come to an end.

Rasoolullah ﷺ **in the Courtyard:** If Rasoolullah ﷺ is seen in someone's courtyard, fire and destruction will visit that place.

A Most Unpleasant Dream: If the Holy Prophet ﷺ is seen as physically deformed or sick or dead then this is a very unpleasant dream. For, it alludes to the observer's negligence and unmindfulness in matters of Deen. Such a person should immediately resort to repentance.

Rasoolullah ﷺ **in Beautiful Garments:** Seeing Rasoolullah ﷺ in beautiful garments implies that the Ummah will attain success materially as well as spiritually.

Seeing Rasoolullah ﷺ **Walking:** Seeing the Holy Prophet ﷺ walking is in reality an instruction from him that the Ummah should engage in Jihaad. It also suggests that the observer of such a dream is negligent in matters of Deen.

Rasoolullah ﷺ **Delivering a Khutbah:** Dreaming of Rasoolullah ﷺ as delivering a khutbah suggests that his Ummah will obey the laws of Shari'ah.

Rasoolullah ﷺ **Looking into the Mirror:** If Rasoolullah ﷺ is seen looking into the mirror it implies that he is urging his Ummah to fully repay whatever *amaanah* (trust) is given to it.

Rasoolullah ﷺ Eating Something: If Rasoolullah ﷺ is seen eating (something) it means he is urging his Ummah to discharge Zakaah.

Rasoolullah ﷺ Presenting a Gift: If someone sees Rasoolullah ﷺ giving him any of his garments to wear or his ring or sword or any other item it means that whatever he acquires (such as land, knowledge, fiqh, the ability to offer constant devotion to Allah) he will acquire it to its maximum.

The Ambiyaa ﷺ: Seeing the prophets of Allah is the same as seeing the angels of Allah Ta'ala suggesting freshness, plentiful rains, reduction of prices of things etc. There is only one exception: the observer will not attain *shahaadah* by seeing the ambiyaa ﷺ as is in the case of seeing the angels of Allah.

Becoming a Nabi: If anyone sees that he has become (any) one of the former apostles of Allah it means that he will be afflicted with similar hardships suffered by that particular Nabi. But he will finally attain success and be granted acceptance in both the worlds. His grief and sorrow will also come to an end.

Ulama and Saints: Much goodness and greatness is attained if one sees the ulama and pious persons in one's dream.

The Ka'bah: The Ka'bah personifies the Imaam or Khalifah of the Muslims. Therefore, any excellence or defects in the Ka'bah reflects similar excellence or defects in the Imaam or Khalifah.

Seeing the Ka'bah in Any Place Other than in Makkah: At times the Ka'bah also stands for peace and harmony. Therefore, if the Ka'bah is seen in a place other than Makkah, it suggests that the people of that town or village will enjoy peace and harmony.

Tawaaf of the Ka'bah: If a person sees himself performing the tawaaf of the Ka'bah or discharging the rites or *manaasik* of Hajj then this is an allusion towards the correctness and authenticity of the Deen he professes.

Viewing the Ka'bah: The mere viewing of the Ka'bah in one's dream means that the observer of the dream will enjoy lasting dignity, exaltedness and victory. For, the Ka'bah is an object of desire for all who have hope.

Placing the Ka'bah Behind One's Back: If a person sees him self placing the Ka'bah behind his back or performing salaah on top of the Ka'bah, it is a sign that he has abandoned Islam.

An Incident: A man once came to Sa'eed ibne Musayyib رحمه الله and said: "I have seen (in my dream) that I am performing salaah on top of the Ka'bah". He replied: "Fear Allah! for it seems to me you have forsaken Islam". The man said: "Your excellency! I hereby offer my repentance in your presence for I have been advocating the beliefs of the Qadriyyah sect since two months."

Performing Salaah in the Ka'bah: If a person sees himself performing salaah in the Ka'bah in the proper manner, observing complete ruku' and sajdah and adopting inner serenity and outer calmness, then it means that he is rightly guided by Allah and steadfast upon the sunnah of Rasoolullah ﷺ. For, salaah is the main pillar of Islam (after Imaan) and a link between Allah and His servant.

But if the salaah is defective, lacking in *khushoo'* and *khudoo'* (ie. inner serenity and outer calmness and composure) it suggests that he has no regard for Islam and his contempt for it is equivalent to the mistakes he makes. He should make amends without further delay.

Inability to Determine the Qiblah: If person sees himself as not being able to determine the Qiblah, it implies that he is confused and astray in matters of religion.

Making Additions to Salaah: And if a person sees himself making additions to the Salaah (such as performing five rak'aat or observing three sajdahs instead of two) then it implies that he has either questioned the authenticity of or entertained doubts with regards the five basic principles of Islam.

Salaah Towards East or West: If a person sees himself performing Salaah, facing east (when qiblah is not in that direction) it means that he will advocate the beliefs of Qadriyyah sect (a sect who believes in the freedom of sill). If he performs Salaah facing west (when Qiblah is not in that direction) it means he will advocate the beliefs of the Jabriyyah (ie. the sect of the fatalists, believing that man has no power of will: he is involuntarily forced by Allah to do good or bad).

Embracing Judaism, Christianity or Fire-Worship: Seeing oneself embracing Judaism, Christianity or the religion of the Fire-worshippers indicates that despite their love and affection for him, he will still oppose and refute them.

Idol Worship: If a person sees himself worshipping idols, it means he will attribute falsehood to Allah Ta'ala propagate falsehood, become a habitual drinker of wine and indulge in sinful acts.

If the idol is of silver it means he will either be in close proximity with sins or he will say falsehood (lie) to his wife.

An idol of gold suggests that he will soon face an unpleasant situation provoking him to become angry.

A wooden idol suggests that he will soon associate with a man who is renegade.

An idol of steel, iron or copper means his single obsession in life is to seek the wealth and pleasures of the world.

Fire Worship: Seeing oneself worshipping fire means the observer will become corrupt in matters of religion. If no flames are seen in the fire, it suggests he will acquire unlawful (haraam) wealth.

Imaamat: Leading a group of people in one's dream suggests that the observer will assume leadership in the community provided he faces towards the proper direction of Qiblah. Such a person will treat his followers with fairness, justness and rectitude. But if he does not face the Qiblah it means he will exploit his subjects during his term of office.

Athaan: Hearing the athaan in one's dream during the months of Hajj (Shawwal, Thil-Qa'dah and 10 days of Thil-Hijjah), means the observer of the dream will perform Hajj. It could also mean he will attain respectability in matters of Deen.

Hearing the Athaan in any Month Other than Thill-Hijjah: If the athaan is heard in any other month besides the months of Hajj it means he will impart the knowledge of Deen through discourses and lectures. The same applies to athaan heard in streets and lanes.

An Incomplete Athaan During the Month of Hajj: Seeing oneself calling out an incomplete athaan during the months of Hajj suggests that the observer of the dream is among the good and pious people. It could also mean he will proceed for Hajj but will not be able to complete it.

An Incomplete Athaan During any Month Other than Hajj: An incomplete athaan during any month other than Thil-Hijjah means he will steal something from which he will not profit at all and, instead, he will become popular as thief.

Calling Out the Athaan in Strange Words: Calling out the athaan in words unknown to the caller suggests that he is a great thief.

A Broken Minaret: A broken or fallen minaret suggests the people of that locality will become corrupt in matters of religion by dividing into numerous sects.

Erecting a Masjid: Erecting or building a masjid is an indication that the person will join a group of people in an effort to accomplish some noble task or to enable someone to get married.

Sneezing: If a person sees himself sneezing in the dream and another says *yarhamukallah* it is tiding that the observer (sneezer) will perform Hajj and Umrah _ insha-Allah.

Shaving the Head: Dreaming of oneself as having shaved one's head during the month of Hajj is a glad tiding that one will proceed for Hajj. But if such a dream is seen during any other month besides Hajj it means that his capital (in monetary terms) will become exhausted. (This will be discussed in greater detail in this book).

Khutbah: If a person sees himself delivering the Khutbah from the mimbar it means he will attain respectability and a vast kingdom on condition that he is worthy of such a position (ie if he is an imaam or a khateeb). But if he is not worthy of such a position it means he will be crucified. In modern times when kingship and crucifixion are hardly in vogue, the same dream could perhaps be interpreted as the bestowment of abundant wealth if he is worthy of such bestowment. If not, he will be condemned to death and perhaps be hanged.

A True Story: It is reported that a person came to Imaam Muhammad bin Sireen رحمة and said: "O Imaam! I dreamt that I was proclaiming the athaan! The Imaam interpreted the dream thus: "Your hands shall be amputated (through stealing)". Then came another person who related a similar dream. The Imaam interpreted his dream thus: "You will proceed for Hajj." The Imaam's students were amazed at theses two conflicting interpretations of two dreams which resembled each other in every respect. They asked for an explanation. He said that he first made a careful study of the character of both the persons and saw signs of evil present in the first person and interpreted his dream accordingly in the light of this verse of the Holy Qur'aan: *Then a claimer proclaimed: O people of the caravan! Surely you are thieves!* As for the second person he saw signs of virtue and piety present in him and therefore, interpreted his dream in the light of the following verse of the Holy Book: *And proclaim (O Ibraheem!) to the people about Hajj!*

The narrator of this incident says: "Matters turned out exactly as the Imaam had interpreted."

At times, athaan could be interpreted as announcement, information and notification.

Reciting the Holy Qur'aan: Looking into the Qur'aan and reciting it depicts Ilm and Hikmah (ie Islamic knowledge and wisdom).

In general, reciting the Qur'aan symbolises truthfulness in speech and conduct.

Section 4 :

Seeing the Skies, Sun, Moon, Stars, Planets, Qiyaamah, Jannah, Jahannam and Fire in One's Dream

Ascending the Sky or Heavens: If a person sees himself as ascending and entering the sky, he will attain martyrdom, become eminent in the sight of Allah, cross the *Siraat* swiftly on the Day of Judgment, attain respectability in this world and be remembered in favourable terms by the people.

Entering the Heavens Without Ascending: If a person sees himself as entering the heavens without ascending, he will first gain honour and respect in this world and then die as a martyr.

The Sun: It represents kingdom and at times, one of both parents.

Holding the Sun: Holding or grasping the sun and having full control over it means that the observer of the dream will acquire dominion (or land) in proportion to the amount he grasps provided the sun is clearly visible and its rays are crystal clear.

If the light and rays of the sun are seen shining on someone the interpretation is the same as above.

Solar Eclipse: A solar eclipse or any change or defect in the sun means similar changes will occur in the observer's domain or the region wherein he lives provided that there is some hint of this the dream. If there is no such hint, it represents one of both parents.

Quarrelling or Disputing with the Sun: Quarrelling and

fighting with the sun suggests that the observer will enter into disputes regarding his domain (or properties) or he will enter into a dispute with one of his parents.

Sunrise in the House: If a person sees the sun rising in his house it is a tiding that he will soon marry if he is a bachelor. Otherwise the kings and rulers will confer great honour upon him.

Clouds Enshrouding the Sun: If the sun is seen covered or shrouded by clouds or anything else, this is an omen that the observer of such a dream will either fall ill or he will become perturbed due to some calamity befalling his estate or one of his parents.

Narration: A person revealed to Imaam Ja'far As-Saddiq (RA) his dream: "I saw the sun rising from my body". The Imaam interpreted the dream thus: "You shall be given abundant wealth and treasures by the king or ruler and they will also confer honour upon you". Another person revealed his dream to the Imaam saying: "I saw the sun rising upon my feet and not any other part of my body". The Imaam interpreted this dream thus: "Wherever you travel, you shall receive from the king or governor wheat, dates and the produce of the land as your livelihood. All these will prove to be most beneficial and profitable for you".

The Moon: Generally the moon symbolises the king's minister or advisor. Sometimes it also symbolises a woman or a handsome lad.

Possessing the Moon: Acquiring possessing or reaching the moon means that the observer of this dream will become advisor to the king or his minister or he will be appointed head of state.

Lunar Eclipse: A lunar eclipse assuming a reddish or dark colour owing to clouds or dust suggests that the person towards whom the moon is linked will soon encounter problems and find himself in some predicament.

Moon in the Lap: If someone dreams of the moon being in his or her lap while he or she is holding it, it is a glad tiding that he or she will be blessed with a boy who will be of much benefit to him or her.

The Moon in the House or Bed: Seeing the moon in one's house or bed is a glad tiding that he will be married to a beautiful woman. The magnitude of her beauty will depend on the magnitude of the moon's beauty. If a lady happens to see such a dream, she will marry a handsome man. Again, his beauty will depend on the beauty of the moon.

The Moon of the First Night of the Lunar Month: If a person sees the crescent of the first night of the lunar month, but in reality it is not the first day of the lunar month, one the following interpretations could be given: (a) he will be entrusted with some duty pertaining to governing of the land or country, (b) a child will be born in his home, (c) a missing person will return, (d) some new event will occur.

The Stars and Planets: As a rule, starts and planets symbolise the nobility or dignitaries of a country. Any goodness in them denote similar goodness in them. Note the interpretations of the following planets:

Mars: It represents the police force, security force and the military force of the king or state.

Saturn: It represents the torturers and interrogators of the king or state.

Jupiter: It either represents the state treasurer or the administrative representative of the state. Sometimes it also represents a man of high learning.

Venus: It represents the queen or wife of the head of state.

Mercury: It represents the secretary of the king or head of state, in charge of all his correspondence.

Possessing the Stars: If a person sees himself as possessing some or many stars it is an indication that he will gain leadership over the notables as well as laity, their number depending on the number of stars he had possessed.

Eating Stars: Eating the stars means he will usurp the wealth of noble persons.

Collecting Stars: Seeing the stars gathered or collected in a certain place means that the observer of the dream will gain leadership of noble personalities thus tending to their needs and fulfilling them.

Stars on the Earth: Stars falling from the sky onto the earth means that part of the earth will be visited with some calamity.

Stars in the Hand: Stars in the hand heralds the birth of a pious boy.

Falling Stars: Stars falling from the sky signifies that if the observer of the dream is wealthy, he will lose all his wealth and become a destitute. And if he is a destitute, he will die as a martyr.

Rotation of the Skies: If the heavens are seen rotating around any person, it suggests that he will be undertaking a journey very soon.

Some true stories relating to this subject are mentioned hereunder:

The First Story: It is reported that once, while Imaam Muhammad Bin Sireen (RA) was having his lunch, a lady came to him and informed him that she had seen a dream. When he asked her to relate it she said: "Not until you have finished your meal". After having had his meal, she said: "I saw the moon entering the planet Taurus and a voice from behind me said to me: *Go to Muhammad Bin Sireen and relate to him your dream!* Hearing this, the Imaam hit his one hand upon the other and said: "Repeat! What did you see?" The lady repeated her dream. Upon this, the Imaam's face turned pale and he got up holding his stomach. His sister came to him asking: "What's the matter with you? Why has your face turned pale?" He said: "Whey should it not when this lady has brought to me the news of my death after seven days? And truly, the Imaam (RA) passed away on the seventh day after this dream. May Allah have mercy upon him.

The Second Story: A man once came to Hazrat Imaam Ja'far (RA) and said: "I saw myself as if I were embracing the moon". The Imaam asked: "Are you a bachelor?" He answered in the affirmative. The Imaam said: "You shall marry the most beautiful lady of her time". Thereafter, the person was not seen for a very long time. Then suddenly he appeared one day and said to the Imaam: "My master! I have married the most beautiful lady of Madeenah. But last night I saw a dream as if I were carrying the moon". The Imaam interpreted this dream saying: "She shall bear you the most beautiful boy of his time". He said: "O master! at this very moment she is expecting". The reporter of this incident says that matters turned out to be exactly as the Imaam had interpreted. May Allah have mercy on the Imaam.

The Third Story: It is related that while the mother of Imaam Shafi' (RA) was expecting him (ie Imaam Shafi'), she saw in her dream as if the planet, Jupiter, left her body and descended on Egypt. Then it started running speedily and its embers spread far and wide and in all the towns and cities of Egypt. The interpretation of this dream was given that a son will be born to her whose knowledge of Deen will be very vast and the people of every town and city of Egypt will benefit from his knowledge and follow his *math-hab*.

Day of Judgement of Qiyaamah: To dream of Qiyaamah having approached means that justice will prevail in that place. The oppressors will be visited with severe punishment from Allah, for, Qiyaamah is referred to as *Youmul-Jazaa* and *Youmul-Fasl* meaning *Day of Retribution* and *Day of deciding who is liable for punishment and who is worthy of reward*. And if the people of that locality are oppressed they will be delivered from their plight.

Standing Before Allah: To see oneself standing before Allah entails a true and genuine dream. Matters will turn out to be very severe for the person. The same applies if a person sees scenes of the horror of Qiyaamah.

Jannah: If a person sees himself entering Jannah it is a glad tiding that he will surely enter Jannah and that his good actions are assuredly accepted by Allah.

Eating the Fruits of Jannah: Seeing oneself eating the fruits of Jannah or giving it to someone else is an excellent dream for the fruits of Jannah symbolise utterance of virtue, excellence and benevolence.

Acquiring But Not Eating the Fruits of Jannah: Acquiring the fruits of Jannah but not eating them or not having the ability to eat them means he will acquire Deen but he will not profit from it. Sometimes a dream of this nature could also mean that he will acquire the knowledge of Deen which will not benefit him in any way.

Streams of Jannah: Drinking from the streams and springs of Jannah means that the observer will have all his legitimate desires fulfilled with dignity in both the worlds.

Garments of Jannah: Dreaming of oneself as having donned the garments of paradise means that the observer will prosper in both the worlds. All his legitimate desires fulfilled in both the worlds.

Gardens, Rivers and Damsels of Jannah: All these suggest that the observer will prosper in both the worlds, the extent of his prosperity depending on how much of the above he sees.

Jahannam or Hell: To see Jahannam in one's dream is a warning that the observer will plunge into commission of heinous crimes and sins. Such a person should immediately resort to *taubah* and refrain from his bad habits and mend his ways.

Admission into Hell: Seeing oneself being admitted into hell is an warning that the observer will plunge into commission of serious crimes. If he sees himself as being unharmed by Jahannam, it is an omen that he will suffer much grief and sorrow, the extent depending on how much he sees.

Fire of the World: A fire in a particular town, suburb or house which is situated on arid land, and such a fire gives off violent, blazing flames destroying anything in its path, and it also gives off thunderous, frightening sounds then such a dream is a bad omen that repression and oppression will become the order of the day in that place where the fire had been seen. If the place is not arid, it means an epidemic, pleurisy or smallpox will break out there or many deaths will occur. If the fire has no sound and flames in it and it destroys some things and leaves other things unharmed, it symbolises accidents and deaths occurring in that place.

Fire Descending from the Skies: Fire descending from the skies is an ominous dream. If such fire does not destroy anything it means the people of that place will verbally quarrel among themselves without causing physical harm. Smoke in such a fire reduces the severity of such a quarrel.

Fire Ascending the Skies: Fire ascending from a particular place towards the skies is also an ominous dream. This means the people of that place have openly declared war with Allah by shamelessly indulging in vice. Moreover, they have levelled allegations and criticism against Allah Ta'ala. Such people should immediately resort to *taubah* and sincere repentance.

Basking Before a Fire: If someone sees himself or another basking before a fire it means he will pursue and thus magnify a certain matter to such an extent that he will profit from it. Consequently, his poverty will come to an end. For, cold symbolises poverty while heat symbolises wealth.

Roasting Meat: If a person sees himself roasting meat on fire, it implies that he will safeguard himself against backbiting.

Eating Roasted Meat: Eating roasted meat means that the observer of the dream will be given meagre livelihood and will face much hardships and anxiety for, roasting is called *shayyun* in Arabic meaning a wound. And a wound causes harm and grief.

Cooking Food in a Pot: Cooking food in a pot on a fire suggests that he will benefit from a house or a matter relating to a house because a pot symbolises the guardian of the house.

An Empty Pot on the Fire: If the pot in which he is cooking is empty it means he will infuriate the guardian or breadwinner of the household or entice him to do something detestable.

Garments Burning: If a person sees his clothes or part of his body on fire it implies that he will encounter some crises relating to his clothes or body. (This will be discussed in greater detail in this book). If such a fire constitutes tongues of flame rising upwards it means harm will come to him from the king or ruler. And if no flames are see it symbolises pleurisy.

Eating Fire: Eating fire which has no flames means he will usurp what is due to orphans. But if such a fire does have flames he will be questioned regarding what is due to orphans. Moreover, people will speak ill of him causing him much agony and mental disturbance.

Scorching by Fire: If someone sees that he is surrounded by flames or flames leap towards him, it suggests that people will backbite about him.

Branding with Fire: Branding with fire means he will hear people cursing and ridiculing him. The greater the branding the greater will be the curse and ridicule.

Sparks: Spark symbolise libelling and defamatory remarks about him. If the sparks are abundant he will soon be afflicted with hardships.

A Burst of Flame in the Hand: A burst of flame in the hand is interpreted as injuries caused to him by the king or ruler.

Fire in the Market Place: Fire seen in the market place or shop is an indication that much loss will be sustained in business.

A Burning Lamp: A powerful bright lamp in the house is a glad tiding that the condition of the inmates of such a house will improve. But any weakness in the light given off by such a lamp denotes similar weakness in their condition. If the lamp extinguishes and no cause for its extinction is known nor is there any hint or any person's death, the observer of the dream will soon encounter difficulties and unpleasant conditions. Also his own condition will change.

Light Given Off by Fire: To burn a fire in the dream and see people being guided by the light of such a fire implies that the person who had enkindled the fire will, through knowledge and wisdom, become a guiding light for the people.

Collecting or Carrying Ashes: Collecting or carrying ashes in the dream means that the person doing so is presently engaged in acquiring futile and worthless knowledge.

Collecting Fire that Does not Burn: Collecting fire which neither burns nor gives of light symbolises knowledge that is futile and worthless.

Section 5:

Dreaming of Rain, Lightning, Thunder, Wells, The Ocean, Rivers, Canals, Vessels, Mills, Winds and Public Baths

Rain: It symbolises assistance and blessings. The same applies to seeing clouds. But if rain or clouds are seen confined to a particular place, house or vicinity, it symbolises famine and sickness or some worldly loss which the people of that place will suffer. In most cases it symbolises difficulties and hardships which will afflict the people of that place.

Rain of Milk and Honey: Rain of butter-oil (ghee), milk, honey or olive oil means the bounties of Allah will abound in that place. Similarly, any rain Wherein there is a hint of goodness means the bestowing of Allah's bounties.

A True Story: Once a person related to Hadhrat Abu Bakar As-Siddeeq رضى الله عنه his dream saying that he dreamt that a cloud sent forth rains of honey and butter-oil (ghee) and there were some who grabbed much of it while others took little of it. Hadhrat Abu Bakr رضى الله عنه interpreted his dream as follows: "As for the cloud, it symbolises Islam. The honey and *ghee* symbolises the sweetness and excellence of Islam. Similarly, any rain comprising of anything beneficial heralds the approaching of good times."

Another True Story: A person said to Imaam Ja'far رحمه الله that he dreamed that he was soaking in the rain for one full day and night. The Imaam exclaimed: "How wonderful a dream you have seen! You are being soaked in the *rahmah* and bounties of Allah. You will be granted peace and *rizq* in abundance".

Another True Story: It was said to Imaam Ja'far ﷺ that a person dreamed that rain was falling particularly on his head. He said: "A very sinful person has seen this dream. Hasn't he heard this verse of the Holy Qur'aan?: *We sent down rains upon them, thus those who were warned, a calamitous rain had fallen on them"*.

Thunder with Wind: It symbolises a cruel and ruthless ruler whose subjects will soon witness his tyranny.

Lightning: For a *musaafir* (traveller) It symbolises fear and danger. And for a *muqeem* (one who is not on a journey) it symbolises hope. This is in view of the verse of the Holy Qur'aan: *It is He (Allah) who shows you lightning as a means of instilling fear (in you, for, such a rain may turn out to be disastrous!) and as a means of instilling hope (in you, for, such a rain may be most fruitful).*

It is said that lightning without rain symbolises impending disaster for both, a *musaafir* as well as *muqeem.*

It is also said that lightning with rain symbolises cure and remedy for a sick person.

A Rainbow: A green rainbow signifies safety from drought and famine. A yellow one symbolises sickness or disease. A red one implies bloodshed. It is said that sometimes the mere dreaming of a rainbow implies that the observer of the dream will marry soon.

Floods: Floods symbolises an attack by the enemy. Rain water flowing in gutters and sewers means prosperity and verdure.

Clouds: It symbolises wisdom, knowledge and blessings. It also implies the Deen of Islam if there is no hint of darkness, windstorm etc.

Possessing, Gathering or Walking in a Cloud: Possessing, gathering, walking in a cloud or mounting a cloud means the observer of the dream will acquire much wealth and prosperity.

A True Story: Imam Ja'far (RA) had been asked about a person who had dreamt that he is eating clouds and there are many clouds before him. He replied that the person had seen a very blessed dream: he will become a man of great learning and by virtue of this he will assume sublimity amongst the people and enjoy a reputation none other has enjoyed.

On another occasion the Imaam had been asked about another person who had seen that he was standing in the shade of a cloud. He replied: "If this person is ill, he will be cured; if he is in debt, he will be absolved of his debt; if he is a destitute, Allah will make him wealth; if he is oppressed, he will receive assistance. For, clouds symbolise *rahmah* (blessings) and anything shrouded by clouds is shrouded by *rahmah*. This is supported by the fact that in times of Jihad clouds used to cast their shadow on Rasoolullah 撒.

Hail, Ice, Frost and Snow: These symbolise sorrow, grief and the punishment of Allah Ta'ala. But, if a small quantity of hail is seen in a place where it normally hails, it heralds verdure and lushness.

Water Becoming Ice: If a person sees that he has taken water by cupping his hands and such water becomes ice it means the wealth he has accumulated will remain intact with him.

Well: A well is normally associated with a person's livelihood and capital. But sometimes it is also interpreted as slyness, cunningness, fraudulence, grief and sorrow.

Digging a well: If a person dreams that he wants to dig a well but is unable to do so it means he will need to toil very hard for his livelihood but will earn very little.

A Well in the House: If a person dreams that he has dug a well in his house or he merely dreams of a well present in his house and such a well swells with water it means that Allah will grant him much *barakah* in his wealth and such wealth will become a means of earning him increased livelihood without much toil and hard work.

In the above case if the well is seen sending forth all its water until it becomes exhausted, it means he will lose much of his wealth with very little remaining.

Irrigating One's Land: If a person sees himself irrigating his land or sprinkling water on his crops it suggests that he will spend his wealth in Allah's way.

Wasting Water: If water is made to flow from a well it means a person will spend his wealth in a manner bringing no benefit or harm to him.

Drawing Water from a Well: If a person dreams that he has drawn water from the well and given it to people to drink, it means he will be a means of providing livelihood to orphans, the weak and poor. It also means he will live a life of piety and virtue. Perhaps his wealth may become a means of people proceeding for Hajj.

Watering a Tree: Drawing water from the well and irrigating the roots of a tree means the person will utilise his wealth in bringing up orphans and educating them.

Giving People Water to Drink: Drawing water from the well and giving it to people to drink means the person doing so will help the people going for Hajj.

Impurities in the Water: Drawing water from the well and seeing impurities and filth in such water means the person doing so will pollute his wealth with *Haraam* wealth.

A Broken Bucket: If the bucket used for drawing water is seen as broken it means the help he used to render to the people will cease.

Sometimes the well is interpreted as cunningness, cheating, grief and sorrow.

Falling into the Well: Climbing down into the well or falling into it means he will be afflicted with grief and sorrow but will eventually witness happiness and joy due to his victory. This is in the light of the story of Hazrat Yusuf عليه السلام.

Plunging into the River: If a person dreams of himself as plunging or entering into a river and thereby panicking or experiencing phobia it means he will soon be afflicted with grief and sorrow.

Drinking Clean Water from the River: Drinking clean water from a river suggests that he will enjoy a certain *ni'mah* and bounty of Allah and live a clean and pure life.

Drinking Unclean Water from the River: If a person sees himself drinking dirty or muddy water from a river it means he will suffer grief, anguish and heartache, the extent depending on the amount he drinks of such water.

Bathing in the River: Bathing in the river or sea and not experiencing any fear, panic or humiliation suggests deliverance from afflictions: if the observer of the dream is grief stricken, his grief will be removed and replaced with happiness; if he is suffering from a disease or sickness, he will be cured; if he is in straitened circumstances, Allah will grant him relief; if he is in straitened debts, Allah will have them fulfilled; if he is imprisoned, Allah will grant him freedom. All this is in the light of this Qur'anic verse wherein He commands Ayyoob ﷺ: *Strike with your foot. This spring of water is for bathing, cooling and drinking. And We granted him his family and doubted their number as a special grace from ourselves and a commemoration for all who have understanding.*

Crossing a River: Crossing a river or stream suggests relief from grief, sorrow and fear. But if such a river or stream contains mud, filth or continues to swell, it suggests the observer of the dream will break off his relationship with his neighbour, son or an intimate friend and establish new relations with someone else. In spite of this he will keep contact with the one with whom his relationship is severed.

The Sea or Ocean: The sea or ocean symbolises a vast kingdom, powerful dynasty provided no filth, muck, sediments or frightening waves are seen.

Drinking Sea Water: If a person dreams that he is drinking sea water and the water is not turbid or muddy nor are any waves seen in such waters it means he will acquire as much of the wealth of this world as the amount of water he had drunk. More over, he shall lead a clean and happy life. But if the water is brackish or filthy or the ocean is shrouded in darkness or the water assumes the for of huge, frightening waves it suggests he will be afflicted with grief, fear and hardship, the intensity of which will depend on how much of the above conditions prevail in the water or ocean.

Drowning: Drowning in the ocean of clean water suggests that the observer of the dream will "drown" in matters of sovereignty or government. But if the water is brackish or filthy it means he will encounter hardships which will cause ruin to him.

Walking on The Sea: Walking on the ocean suggests he will have dominance on the nobility and elite people of the world.

Vessel or Ship: A sea-going vessel normally symbolises deliverance and safety from calamities. Sometimes it is interpreted as a means of reaching the king or becoming intimate with him or serving him. At times it is also interpreted as grief and anxiety which will ultimately come to an end.

Boarding or Sitting in a Vessel: If a person sees himself as having boarded a vessel which is sea-bound or merely cruising on water it suggests that he will become entangled with the king or authorities carrying out an investigation on him. The seriousness of the investigation will depend on the capacity of the vessel. Ultimately he will be liberated from their clutches.

Water in the Vessel: Boarding or sitting in a vessel filled with water suggests grief, sorrow, anxiety, calamity, imprisonment or sickness. But the ultimate result will be deliverance and salvation.

Disembarking a Vessel: Disembarking or leaving a vessel indicates swift deliverance from any calamity.

Vessel on Dry Land: If a person sees a vessel approaching him, it is a glad tiding that he will soon find solutions to his problems and be delivered from anxieties.

Stream: A stream or small river wherein a person normally does not drown is the same as a river except that in most cases it symbolises a glad tiding and a clean, joyful life.

A Stream in the House: A clean stream with sweet water flowing in or through the house symbolises a pure and clean life. But if the water is seen in the form of a spring emitting from within the walls or any such place from which the flowing of water is regarded as strange and absurd, it suggests that the folks of that settlement will be visited with some calamity causing them much grief, sorrow, fear and weeping, the intensity of which will depend on the force of the water gushing out from such a spring Likewise, matters will be more serious if the water is foul, brackish or muddy. Drinking such water suggests he will be afflicted with profound grief proportionate to the amount of water he drinks.

Wudhu and Ghusl: Performing wudhu or ghusl with water from a stream or small river suggests one of the following: if the observer of the dream is grief-stricken, Allah will grant him happiness; if he is living in fear, Allah will grant him safety and security; if he is in debts Allah will provide him with the means to fulfil his debt; if he is sinful, Allah will conceal his sins, grant him pardon and atonement; if he is ill, Allah will grant him complete cure. This interpretation is in the light of the story of Hazrat Ayyub ﷺ.

Water in a Dish or Bowl: If a person dreams of himself as holding or possessing water contained in a dish or bowl and he is conscious of himself as being in a state of *tuhr* (ie. ceremonial purity) or on a journey in an unknown and strange place, then such a bowl of water symbolises his life span. If he dreams of drinking all the water it means his life span is completed: he should now prepare for the hereafter. If he drinks the water partially it means he still has a number of years to live. The same interpretation is given if, instead of water, the contents of the bowl or dish is *thareed* ★.

★ Thareed: Pieces of bread steeped in broth.

Drinking Water: Consuming clean, sweet water in the dream means he will enjoy a clean and happy life provided he does not know its quantity nor is he aware of himself being in a state of *tuhr* nor does he know himself to be n a journey in a strange, unknown place. The same applies if the water is not sweet. But if the water is brackish and muddy, it means he will suffer from some ailment or disease whose seriousness will depend on how brackish or muddy the water is.

Water in a Glass Tumbler: A tumbler or glass symbolises one's wife and the water symbolises a son provided one does not drink the water. If a person sees himself as watering an orchard or irrigating a land from the water contained in such a tumbler, it means his matrimonial life will be one of happiness and prosperity. Then, if he sees the orchard or land yielding fruits or crops it means his wife will bear him children. But if he sees someone else watering his orchard or land it is a dream which is regarded as abominable and loathsome.

Wudhu and Ghusl with Milk, Wine, Oil etc.: If a person sees himself performing wudhu or ghusl with milk, wine, oil or any such liquid or fluid with which wudhu and ghusl are not valid, it means his worldly and religious pursuits will not be fulfilled.

Incomplete Wudhu: An incomplete wudhu with ordinary clean water suggests that the observer's worldly and religious pursuits will remain incomplete. But as opposed to wudhu with milk, wine etc, matters will be less harsh. The same applies with salaah which is incomplete.

Complete Wudhu or Ghusl: A complete wudhu or ghusl suggests complete pardon from sins and evil.

Soil and Mud: These symbolises grief, sorrow and fear. Their magnitude depends on how much soil or mud is seen.

Hot Water: Hot water suggests grief caused by a king, ruler or government authorities. The hotter the water the more intense the affliction. At times, hot water also symbolises fear, consternation or sickness.

Brick: A brick which is baked or dried in the sun so that it is no longer clay, usually symbolises one's wealth which one had accumulated. Acquiring a portion of a brick suggests that the observer of the dream will acquire accumulated wealth.

A Brick Falling from a Wall: A brick falling from a wall means a male or female member of his family will either get lost or run away or pass away.

Bathroom: A bathroom or hot bath symbolises grief caused by women. But since a person normally spends very little of his time in the bathroom it means his grief will be short-lived.

Urinating in a Bathroom: Urinating in a bathroom or removing hair with lime or any shaving cream is regarded as a good dream: if in misery, the observer will soon find relief from his misery; if in fear, he will soon find happiness; if grief-stricken, his grief will soon be removed; if he is ill, he will soon recover and enjoy good health. If none of the above condition _ meaning that if he is not ill, he will become ill; if he is happy, he will be afflicted with grief, perhaps caused by some financial loss.

A General Rule Pertaining to a Dream with Two Scenes with Opposing Interpretations: When two separate things with opposing interpretations are seen in a dream then the stronger or better of the two interpretations will be given. As an example if a person sees a bathroom and himself as removing hair using a lotion or lime _ whereas a bathroom represents grief and sorrow and removing hair using a lotion or lime represents the removing of grief and sorrow _ it means that his grief and sorrow will be removed, for the dream of removing hair using lime or lotion is regarded as stronger or better.

Grinding Stones: If a person sees a grinding stone in motion, it signifies that he will most definitely acquire sustenance but afer much difficulty and hardship, but such sustenance will be pure and *halaal*. If a grinding stone is seen grinding wheat thus producing flour, it means the observer will acquire sustenance as a result of someone else's toil. But if he, himself operates the grinding stone, it means he will earn his own livelihood.

Sometimes, a mill or grinding stone represents fighting or quarrelling if there is anything to suggest this in the dream.

Winds and Storms: Normal blowing of wind without any sign of darkness heralds blessings and *barakah* as suggested by this verse of the Holy Qur'aan: *And it is He (Allah) who sends the winds like heralds of glad tidings, going before His mercy.* But is such winds resemble storms, typhoon etc. they suggest grief, sorrow and perplexities as is known from the following verse of the Holy Qur'aan: *And in the people of Aad there was another sign when We sent against them a wind barren of any goodness.*

Section 6 :

Seeing the Earth, Mountains, Deserts, Hills, Structures, Forts, Shops, Houses, Buildings, Explosions, Earthquakes etc. in One's Dream

The Earth: Its interpretation is very diverse: for example, if its boundary is visible in the dream it symbolises a woman; if not it symbolises worldly affairs; if it abounds in some unknown vegetation, it symbolises the Deen of Islam. The same applies to deserts. These are only two examples. Read on to learn more about it.

Standing in Vast Stretch of Land: Standing in the middle of a vast stretch of land suggests that a wonderful and peaceful life awaits him. It also means safety, protection, peace and harmony.

A Narrow Piece of Land: If the land is restricted it means the end of his life. The same dream could perhaps mean *wilaayah* if the beholder of such a dream is worthy of it. *Wilaayah* could be interpreted as *the office of sainthood*, dominion, sovereignty jurisdiction and the like.

Dialogue with the Earth: To see the earth speaking to a person indicates that he will acquire such prosperity that will cause people to be amazed and astonished. The same interpretation is given when such a thing is seen speaking to a person which does not possess the faculty of speech.

Disappearance into the Earth: If a person sees himself disappearing into the earth without a grave it means he will ruin himself because of his obsession in worldly pursuits. If the disappearance is in a hole or grave, it means he will encounter something extremely offensive as a result of committing a crime or by being cheated.

The Earth Revolving: If a person sees the earth causing him to go round and round, it means his affairs will be left in total disarray and confusion: he will thus flee from one place to another in pursuit of his livelihood.

Traversing through Wasteland, Wilderness or the Desert: If a person sees himself traversing through wasteland, wilderness or desert in such a manner that he does not get lost it means he will remain steadfast upon the religion of Islam. If he gets lost it means he is in doubt about Islam.

Eating and Drinking in the Wild: This suggests that he will acquire affluence in the world and progress in matters of Deen.

Soil and Sand: Soil, sand and dust symbolises wealth in the form of goods. If someone sees soil, sand or dust flying on him or he sees himself eating it, it suggests that he will become wealthy and affluent.

Walking on Sand or Picking Up Sand: If a person sees himself walking on sand or picking up sand, it means he will have to toil very hard in order to become wealthy.

Sand or Dust Flying in the Atmosphere or Skies: Sand or dust flying in the atmosphere or skies symbolises the beholder's affairs becoming chaotic. The same interpretation is given if mist or fog is seen.

Digging the Earth: If someone sees himself digging the earth and eating the soil, it means he will acquire wealth by cheating and deceiving people.

A True Incident: It is narrated that Rabee'ah bin Umayyah bin Khalf came to Hadhrat Abu Bakr As-Siddeeq ﷺ and said: "O Khaleefah of the Messenger of Allah, I saw a dream last night. I saw my self in a lush and green land. Then I suddenly saw myself in a barren land. At this stage I saw you clasping your neck with both your hands".

Hadhrat Abu Bakr As-Siddeeq ﷺ said: "If what you are saying is true then I am afraid you will forsake the Deen of Islam. As for me all my affairs will remain protected and my hands will not be contaminated through worldly pursuits".

The narrator says that during the Khilaafat of Hadhrat Umar ﷺ Rabee'ah left Madinah to live in Rome. There he embraced Christianity in the presence of the then king and died as one.

Mountains and Hills: Mountains and hills represent people, their ranks and positions depending on the hugeness, height and mass of such mountains and hills. The same applies to boulders and rocks. The person who sees such a dream will attain honour and dignity.

Climbing a Mountain: If a person sees himself climbing a mountain it means he will attain high positions.

Rocks and Stones: These symbolise hardness of heart, cruelty, harshness and haughtiness.

Pebbles: Pebbles symbolise backbiting and levelling allegation against someone.

Standing On Top of a Mountain: If a someone sees himself standing on top of a mountain, it means he will overpower another person with a similar rank or position such as his.

Conquering or Dropping a Mountain: If a person sees himself conquering or defeating a mountain (as in a fight), it means he will commit murder.

Digging a Hole in the Mountain: If a person sees himself breaking into the mountain (just as a thief breaks into a house) or digging into the mountain, it means he is guilty of deceiving someone.

Ascending a Mountain without Faltering: If someone sees himself climbing a mountain without faltering, it is a hint that his desire to acquire a particular thing will be fulfilled _ but after much difficulty and hardship.

Ascending: Seeing oneself ascending ordinarily (as in real life) means one will attain honour, dignity and an elevated position. Such ascension is indeed, an enviable one. In general, ascension or climbing represents one's honour and dignity in worldly and religious matters. At other times, climbing a mountain or tree suggests that the beholder will be granted protection against calamities of all sorts.

Carrying a Mountain: The carrying of stones, rocks and mountains means one will be made to carry great burdens by people who are hard and cruel.

Shops and their Frontage: Shops and pavements where merchandise is normally sold symbolises merchandise and goods. But pavements and terraces which are not normally occupied for trading purposes, but instead are utilised for converging, means that the beholder will plunge into lengthy discussions.

An Unknown House: If a person sees himself in a house whose foundation, location and occupants are not known to him, it symbolises his abode in the Hereafter Every feature of such a house _ eg. narrowness, spaciousness, ugliness, beauty _ is an identical replica of his abode in the Hereafter. Subsequently, this is a reflection of his deeds and actions in the world.

A Known House: If he sees a house which is known to him, it symbolises his position and condition in this world. Its features _ be they pleasant or unpleasant, such as the house being straight or crooked, spacious or narrow, orderly or disorderly _ is a reflection of his behaviour and character.

Possessing a House: If a person sees himself owning a house known to him it suggests that the will acquire worldly gains proportionate to the spaciousness, attractiveness and elegance of such a house.

An Extended House: Seeing one's house or its foundation

extended means that beholder's wealth and assets will in crease in proportion to the extension.

A Ruined House: Seeing one's house in ruins or raised to the ground means that his future will be ruined as a result of his evil deeds.

Selling a House: Seeing oneself selling one's house is inactive of the termination of his life.

Building a House in an Unknown Locality: The building of a house in an unknown locality suggests that the beholder will accomplish good deeds and that he will secure for himself a favourable position in the Hereafter.

Demolishing a House: If a person sees himself demolishing an unknown house, it suggests that all his previous anxieties have been removed and that all his sins and evil doings are revoked. But if the house is known to him, it suggests that he will lose all his worldly possessions due to his evil doings and squandering. If only a portion of his house is demolished it means he will suffer worldly loss proportionate to how much is demolished.

Mansion: A mansion in a city with huge windows is regarded as an excellent dream. Climbing such a mansion means the beholder will attain lofty positions during his lifetime. Good fortune and happiness are in store for him.

A Wall: A wall reflects the status and position of a person if he is seen standing on top of it. But if he sees himself falling from the wall, it means he is heading for destruction.

A Plastered or Cemented House: A house which is plastered symbolises a grave. If a person sees himself imprisoned in a new, plastered house which is unknown to him then such a house represents his grave.

An Unplastered House: An unknown and unplastered house symbolises a woman.

Climbing the Upper Portions of a House: If a person sees himself entering an unknown house and climbing the upper portions of the house, it means he will marry some woman who will be a means of prosperity for him.

A Familiar House: If a person sees himself owning a house which is not strange to him, it means he will soon find a wife for himself. Sometimes, the mere seeing of a house suggests a person's material wealth and assets.

Sweeping a House: The sweeping of one's own house means that poverty is in store for him. The sweeping out of another's house means he will acquire much wealth from the owner of that house.

Digging a Grave: The digging of a grave means he will build a house.

A City in Ruins: The total or partial devastation of a city suggests that the inhabitants of that city will forsake their Deen. They may even lose their accumulated resources as a result of their misdeeds.

Ladder of Stairs: Climbing a ladder or stairs symbolises the religion of Islam by virtue of which he will acquire high stations in the Hereafter.

Stairs of Unbaked Bricks: Climbing stairs constructed of unbaked bricks suggests that he will enjoy honour in the world by giving charity.

Stairs of Baked Bricks, Timber or Mortar: Climbing any of these suggests that he will attain high status in the world provided there is something in the dream to suggest this.

A Door: It symbolises the head of the household and at other times the one who manages the household affairs which is, in most cases, one's wife. Any pleasant or unpleasant condition in such a door bespeaks of a similar condition in her. For example, a broken, displaced or burnt door could mean dispute or separation between wife and husband.

The Lintel: The upper lintel or doorframe symbolises the husband while the lower one, the wife.

A Gutted House: If a person sees his house devastated by fire it is a hin that he will disgraced by an authority; or he will be afflicted by an epidemic disease.

A Displaced Door: A displaced door is a hint that the head of the household will die.

A Dislodged Door or Doorframe: If the door or doorframe of one's house is seen dislodged, it means the lady who owns the house or the landlady will die.

Someone Sitting on a Dislodged Door: If a person sees the door of his house displaced or dislodged and another person sitting on it, it means he will sell his house and his wife will marry someone else.

A Door Falling: A door seen falling indicates that the beholder will first become ill then regain his health.

Doorframes: The timber with which doorframes and lintels are made represent one's children. If two sides of a doorframe is seen broken, it means his two daughters will die. But if he has more than two daughters, it means all of them will get married, thereby leave his home permanently to live with their husbands.

Closing the Door: If a person sees himself closing the door of his house it means he will divorce his wife.

Opening a Closed or Locked Door: If the house whose door is being opened is known to him it means he will marry. If not, it means his Dua's will be granted.

A Nail: A nail symbolises a person who assists people in solving their problems.

A Bridge: A bridge has the same interpretation as a nail.

Earthquakes and Tremors: These are forewarnings of certain major happenings in the world. A quake on mountains points towards evil Ulama. A quake on one's own body suggests that one is bereft of all goodness and worthiness. A tremor in one's house suggests that his house will become a venue for adultery. To see an entire house or part of it in ruins as a result of a tremor is an indication that the owner's life will terminate shortly.

Section 7:

Seeing Trees, Gardens, Orchards, Fruits Vegetable, Crops, etc. in the Dream

Trees: Trees symbolise men in personality and character. If a person dreams that he has received fruit or leaves of a specific tree, it means he will receive abundant wealth from such a person who resembles that particular tree in personality and character.

Timber and Firewood: Hard timber implies hypocrisy in habits or in matters relating to Deen. The same implies to firewood, small or big, dry or green.

Twigs: Twigs normally used to start a fire mens that backbiting, tale-bearing and slandering will become rife amongst the people.

Staff (*Asaa*): A staff such as the one used by a *khateeb* when delivering a khutbah symbolises a dignified, trustworthy and reliable person who has leadership qualities and is worthy of being followed.

A Thorn Tree: If a thorn-tree is seen in the dream, it means the observer of the dream will suffer some harm caused by some person. It could also be a forewarning of an impending calamity.

Vineyard: It symbolises a woman. If a person sees himself planting a grape tree and it has grown tall so that it provides shade, it means he will attain honour and dignity. The same dream could also be a glad tiding that his child will live and grow up health. If it is only one tree, it is a glad tiding that he will receive money equivalent to one thousand Dirhams.

Pomegranate During its Season: If it is sweet, it symbolises one's accumulated wealth.

Eating a Sweet Pomegranate: Whether eaten entirely or partially, it means he will receive assets, leaving him richer and wealthier than before.

Sour Pomegranate: If a sour pomegranate is eaten, it means he will be afflicted with grief and sorrow. The same applies to any sour fruit.

Apples: It symbolises a man's trade, his income as well as his courage. Hence, if a king sees himself eating it, it symbolises his kingdom. If a trader sees it, it symbolises his trade. Therefore, if a person sees himself as acquiring or eating one, it means he will acquire wealth proportionate to the freshness, taste and extent of the apple he has eaten: if it was sweet, the wealth will be excellent; if fresh, it will be of good quality; if little, he will acquire little; if a great deal, he will acquire it in abundance.

Oranges: Oranges, if many, they symbolises lawful wealth. If only three or less, they symbolises lawful wealth. If only three or less, they symbolise righteous children. There is no harm in seeing the yellow portion of an orange.

Yellow Fruit: Seeing yellow fruit such as apples, apricots, pears, saffron etc. in one's dream implies that the observer of his dream will fall ill.

Green Fruit: If green fruit is seen, it suggests wealth which will be of no benefit to the observer.

Watermelon: A green fruit one symbolises livelihood. A yellow one symbolises illness if it is eaten.

Bananas: Bananas of any species or type, in season or out of season, symbolise goodness and prosperity. If an ordinary person sees it, it suggests an increment in his wealth. If a person who adheres firmly to the Deen sees it, it suggests that he will make further progress in his Deen.

Grapes: If these are seen during the grape season, it is an excellent dream. If seen out of season, it symbolises illness.

Eating a Specific Number of Grapes: If a person sees himself eating specific number of grapes (ie. he counts them while eating them) it suggests that he will either be given the same number of lashes or the same number of pimples on his body.

Black Grapes: Black grapes, although in reality are excellent, but in a dream they do not augur well for the one who sees them. The reason being that Hadhrat Nooh عليه السلام cursed his son out of anger. Consequently, the grapes that the son had in his hand turned black. Therefore, in view of this incident there is no benefit in seeing black grapes.

Pressing Grapes: If a person see himself pressing grapes, it means that he will serve the king or ruler.

Pressing Olives: The interpretation is the same as pressing grapes.

Olive Oil: Possessing Olive oil or any other pleasant smelling oil heralds blessings. prosperity and wealth.

Black or Red Raisins: They signify blessings, prosperity, livelihood and wealth.

Figs: They represent grief and sorrow due to the fact that Hadhrat Aadam عليه السلام sat under a fig tree after his expulsion from Jannah.

Walnuts: It means quarreling. Otherwise it means livelihood obtained after much exertion.

Almonds and Pistachios: Green or dry, both indicate hidden wealth. Or livelihood which the observer will obtain from unknown sources.

Hazelnuts: It symbolises wealth in abundance which th observer will obtain.

Non-fruit-bearing Trees: They symbolise a person who is of little or no benefit.

Sweet-Smelling Trees: The observer will meet a man of honour, integrity and respect.

Odorous Trees: A tree giving off bad smell symbolises an evil person whom the observer will encounter.

Wheat: Eating green wheat signifies that the consumer will progress in matters of Deen and will obtain lawful sustenance. Eating dry or cooked wheat is of no real significance as inferred from the incident of Hadhrat Aadam ﷺ.

Barley: Whether fresh or dried, cooked or baked, eaten or merely possessed, all symbolise lawful sustenance.

Flour: Flour made of wheat or barley symbolises a person's wealth which he had amassed. It means a life of ease and prosperity lies ahead of him. Eating flour is better than bread since bread is subjected to the heat of fire.

Bread or *Roti* Made of Flour: It symbolises excessive wealth. Prosperity and a comfortable life is in store for the one who eats it.

Dough: Seeing dough in one's dream heralds many children whom the observer will father. If he own fruit trees, it means the tree will bear fruit in abundance.

Kneading Dough: If a person sees himself kneading dough it means he will father a great many children and his trees will bear excessive fruit and his land will yield plentiful food _ but after much toiling and hard work.

Rice: It symbolises wealth which the observer is after and which he will obtain after toiling hard.

Sesame: It symbolises one's ever increasing wealth. No deficiency will plunder such wealth.

Corn and Millet: Each symbolises one's wealth which will be of no avail to one.

Beans: It means prolonged grief and sorrow.

Chickpeas *(Chana)*, **Lentils** *(Masoor)* **and Peas:** Seeing any of these means the person will obtain unlawful wealth after much grief and sorrow.

A Field Meant for Growing Produce: Seeing his fields utilised for growing produce means that he will prosper in matters pertaining to his Deen and worldly life. The greener the field the greater the prosperity.

Reaping a Field: It alludes to bloodshed.

Sewing Seeds: The one who plants the seeds will accomplish good work or he will be engaged in doing social work.

Seeds Grown into Plants or Trees: It is a glad tiding that his good deeds are accepted by Allah Ta'ala and that he will attain popularity, credibility and dignity in this world as a result of his good actions. At other times seeds may be interpreted as one's children on condition that the field wherein the seeds are sewn is seen in its entirely and he is familiar with it.

Vegetable: Cucumbers, turnip and other greens symbolise meagre sustenance which the observer will acquire after experiencing grief and fear. At times, it could also mean that one's grief and sorrow will intensify and the obtaining of *rizq* will prolong. The same is the interpretation of coconut, onions, leek, garlic, ginger, carrots, radish etc.

Sweet Smelling Flowers: Fragrant flowers such as roses, jasmine, narcissus, marigold, daisies etc. _ if any of these are seen detached from its stem _ it suggests that the observer will lose his accumulated wealth. But if they are not, it is a harbinger of a son who will be good, honest and righteous. How righteous he will be depends on the intensity of the fragrance given of by such a flower.

Unknown Greenery: The growing of any unknown greenery in a place where it does not normally grow such as a house or masjid, suggests that man will come along either to seek in marriage the hand of his daughter or to establish a business partnership with him.

Dry Grass: Dry grass serves as a harbinger for receiving gold in the near future. Imaam Muhammad Bin Sireen ﷜ used to refer to grass as pure gold. Once, when he was presented with a camel load of dry grass, he looked at it for a long time, then said: "I wish I had seen this in my dream!", for then he would have received gold.

Garden: A garden is interpreted as the observer's wife.

Eating Fruits in the Garden: It means the observer will receive wealth from a wealthy woman.

Pleasure in the Garden: Merriment or a pleasure walk in a garden suggests that he will meet up with a beautiful woman with whom he will live happily.

Broken Gate of a Garden: If one side of the gate leading to the garden is seen as broken, it means the observer will divorce his wife.

An Unknown Garden: It stands for Jannah. Entering and touring such a garden suggests that the observer will attain Jannah by way of making greater progress in matters of Deen.

Section 8:

Dreaming of Milk and Other Beverages

Milk: Milk in general symbolises the *Fitratul Islam* and the *Sunnah of Rasoolullah* 騣. *Fitratul Islam* means the natural religion of Islam while *Sunnah* means the actions of Rasoolullah 騣. Thus, drinking or possessing milk suggests that the observer will attain righteousness and he will remain steadfast on his Deen.

Drinking Fresh Milk: If a person sees himself drinking fresh milk (not whey or curd) of a known animal, it implies that he will acquire wealth that is halaal and lawful.

Drinking Curd or Whey: Drinking any of these means loss of wealth as a result of which he will be grieved.

Cheese: It symbolises happiness, prosperity and assets in general. Fresh cheese is regarded better than dried cheese.

Cow Milk, Camel Milk and Buffalo Milk: All three symbolise prosperity and goodness. Sheep milk also symbolises prosperity and goodness but to a lesser degree than the former.

Milk of Wild Camel: It symbolises progress in one's Deen.

Mule Milk: If drunk, it symbolises terror and hardship.

Donkey Milk: A tamed donkey's milk represents serious illness but he will be cured.

Milk of Game: Milk of all edible game symbolises prosperity and lawful *rizq*.

Horse Milk: The drinker will acquire a good reputation.

Lioness Milk: It means the observer will defeat his foe.

Milk of Bitch: It represents intense fear and that the observer's foe will gain victory over him.

Vixen Milk: Vixen or she-fox milk symbolises goodness, well being, happiness and prosperity.

Sow's Milk: The one who drinks it, his mentality and thinking will change for the worse.

Drinking Milk from the Breast: If a person sees himself drinking or being fed milk from the breast of a woman, it means he will either be imprisoned or find himself in utter poverty, as the maximum period for suckling is two years. Anything beyond that means imprisonment or dire straits.

Breast filling with Milk: If a woman sees her breast filling with milk or milk flowing from her breasts, it is interpreted as prosperity and wealth in abundance coming her way.

Wine: It symbolises unlawful wealth if there is no suggestion of any dispute with someone over the wine. But if there is any such suggestion then it is some harm coming his way.

Intoxicants Made from Dates or Grapes: They signify apprehension and doubt about one's resources or about the lawfulness of one's earnings.

Intoxication: Intoxication without drinking wine suggests something unfavourable, for Allah Ta'ala says: *You shall see mankind as drunk, yet they are not drunk: but (the truth is that) the punishment of Allah is dreadful.*

Drinking Wine: Drinking wine with another means the drinker will quarrel with that person with regards to his livelihood provided there is a dining table between them.

Brewing Wine: The brewer will be employed by the king or the ruler and great decisions will be made by him.

River of Wine: If a person sees a river flowing with wine and such a river flows through lush and green land with which he is not familiar, drinking from such a river or entering such land is a glad tiding that the observer will attain Jannah. But if he does not consumed such wine or does not enter such land, it forewarns an impending calamity.

Honey: Honey symbolises pure and lawful wealth and cure from sicknesses.

Section 9 :

Dreaming of Men, Women and Animals

Conversing or Receiving Something from a Known Person: To see someone speaking to the observer or giving him something suggests that the observer will socialise or deal with him or someone who bears a similar name or resembles him.

Seeing an Unknown Person: An unknown person represents an enemy if he is young. But if he is old, it suggests the observer's good fortune and success in whatever he is pursuing currently.

An Old Man: If an old man is seen speaking to him or giving him something, it means he will succeed in whatever he is pursuing. If the old man is of a pleasant personality and good looks, it means his pursuit is of a favourable nature. Otherwise, it is of an unfavourable nature. Otherwise, it is of unfavourable nature.

An Old Woman: If unknown, she symbolises the current the year. If she is beautiful, the year will bring good fortune. If ugly, the year will prove a disaster.

A Young Girl: If she is not known to him, she symbolises his current year. Further, if she is beautiful and healthy and she is seen speaking to him or giving him something or he sees himself hugging her or making love to her or having intercourse with her it means the current year will prove profitable and fruitful for him. If not beautiful, the year will prove a disaster.

A Newborn Girl: It is deemed a better dream than a newborn boy. It symbolises joy and happiness for the one who sees her.

A Newborn Boy: It suggests grief and hardships for the one to whom a boy is born.

Eunuchs: To see castrated males who are unknown is tantamount to seeing the angels.

Head: The head represents the observer's leader or portion. This could well be his father, brother, employer, chief, husband, king etc. Thus, any defect in the head points to a similar defect in the leader or patron. Sometimes the head represents a person's capital.

A Dismembered Head: To see one's head detached from the body without being struck suggests one of the following: that one's leader or patron will break off his relationship with him; or the observer will lose his capital; or his present means of livelihood will come to an end.

The Hair of the Head: Hair symbolises a man's wealth and assets or that f his employer's

Shaving the Head: If a person sees himself shaving the head in any month other than the Months of Hajj★ or the Sacred Months★★, either his capital will be lost or that of his employer's; or he will lose his job. If seen during the months of Hajj, it could only mean something good coming his way: perhaps he will proceed for Hajj.

Long Hair: Seeing the hair as long, one of the following interpretations could be given: if he is a soldier, his strength, elegance and awe will increase; if he is a Hashimite, he will gain leadership in his community; if the observer is a businessman, his merchandise will increase; if he is a farmer his crops will increase.

Dishevelled Hair: Hair which has grown long, covering the face forewarns grief and sorrow.

White Hair: Seeing one's black hair turning white in the dream means that he will gain credibility and respect among his people.

★   Months of Hajj: Shawwaal, Zil-Qa'dah, Zil-Hijjah.

★★   Sacred Months: Zil-Qa'dah, Zil-Hijjah, Muhharram, Rajab.

Black Hair: Seeing one's white hair turning black suggests that his present condition will be transformed.

The Face and Beard: The face and beard symolises a man's status and awe. Seeing one's beard lengthened suggests that his position or status will be elevated.

A Long Beard: An abnormally long beard means grief, sorrow and impending calamity.

A Shaven Beard: To see the beard being shaven means that he will lose his dignity and respectability amongst the people. The same is the interpretation of the hair of the beard falling off.

Removing the Hair of the Head and the Beard Simultaneously: If there is anything to suggest any goodness in such a dream it means that if observer is in difficulty, Allah will remove it; if he in debt, Allah will enable him to pay it; if he is ill, Allah will grant him cure. But if here is no suggestion of any good then the dream is not of a favourable nature.

Dyeing the Hair of the Head: Dyeing the hair symbolises concealment and protection. Thus, if a person sees himself dyeing his hair it means that Allah will protect him from the evil consequences of what he intends to do. But if the dye does not stick to his hair, it means he will not be granted protection.

Rubbing Oil on the Hair, Beard or Body: Normal oiling of the hair, beard or body suggests beauty and elegance. But if excessive oil is seen flowing on the face or clothes, it suggests grief and sorrow.

Fragrant Oil: Rubbing sweet-smelling oil amplifies one's beauty and elegance.

Smoke: It symbolises praises and compliments coupled with terror an danger as smoke means danger from a ruler or authority.

Seeing Hair on the Palm: The growing of hair on the palm or any such place where hair does not grow suggests that he will incur debts which will shatter his peace, causing him extreme anxiety.

Hair of the Armpits, Pubic Hair and the Moustache: If the hair is small or few, it symbolises steadfastness on Deen and Sunnah. If the hair is plenty it symbolises *wilaayat* which is bereft of Deen.

Hair of the Human Body: It symbolises a man's assets. If he has merchandise or crops, it will increase or decrease according to the amount of hair he had seen. If he sees the hair shining he will become a destitute if he is wealth. Or he will become wealthy if he is a destitute; if he is perturbed, he will become pleased; if he is ill, he will be cured; if he is in debt, it will be paid.

Urine: It is the same as seeing the hair of the human body.

Human Brain: It symbolises a person's wealth and assets. Eating the brain in the dream suggests that he is living off his own lawful earnings. Eating someone else's brain or an animal's brain suggests that he is living off someone else's earnings.

Human Flesh: If cooked or roasted it symbolises wealth. if uncooked it means backbiting – if eaten. For Allah Ta'ala says: *Would any of you like to eat the flesh of his dead brother? Nay you will abhor it.*

The Ear: The ear symbolises a person's wife or daugher. If the ear is seen not functioning (or as dead) it means he will divorce his wife or she will die. It could also means his daughter will get married.

Embellishment of the Ear: Seeing the ear adorned with jewellry of any sort serves as a glad tiding that his daughter or wife are living a tranquil and happy life.

The Faculty of Hearing: It symbolises a person's Deen. Thus, if a person sees his hearing ability increased it suggests that he will progress in matters of Deen. But if he sees it as defective, it suggests similar defects in his Deen.

Voice: It symbolises his popularity amongst people. The louder and the more beautiful his voice, the greater the popularity he will enjoy.

The Eye: It symbolises his Deen and his rightful conduct. The same applies to his ability to see. Any defect in the eye or the faculty of sight bespeaks of similar defect in his Deen. Any excellence in the eye or the faculty of sight bespeaks of similar excellence in his Deen.

Applying *Kuhl* or *Surma* to the Eye: Applying *surma* to the eyes suggests the observer's rightful conduct in matters of his Deen. Applying *surma* in the eyes with the object of adornment suggests that the observer will accomplish a religious task as a result of which he will enjoy credibility amongst the people. Sometimes a person's eye may symbolise either his belongings, son, brother or leader. Any excellence or defect in the eye will then reflect a similar excellence or defect in any of the above.

Eyebrows and Eyelashes: They symbolises the preservation of one's Deen and the heeding of its message. The healthier they are the greater its preservation and the more he will respond to its message.

The Nose and Forehead: They symbolises a person's status, honour and dignity. Any excellence or defect in them bespeaks of similar excellence or defect in his status, honour and dignity.

The Temples, Cheeks and Jaws: They symbolises his method of earning his livelihood. If they are sound his livelihood will be earned without difficulty. If they are defective then it will be earned with much difficulty.

The Lips: They symbolise the assistance he receives from people. The upper lip is regarded better than the lower one.

The Tongue: It symbolises his spokesperson and messenger. At other times it symbolises the soundness of his argument. Thus, if he sees his tongue as cut or short, it suggests that his argument regarding a certain dispute is weak. And if there is no such dispute, it symbolises his steadfastness on Deen. As opposed to the above, if he sees his tongue as elongated, it suggests that his argument is sound enough to make him gain victory over his opposition. And if there is no such dispute, it alludes to his habit of indulging in idle talk as well as his shamelessness. A woman's tongue seen as shortened or cut is always regarded as favourable.

The Front Two Teeth _ Upper and Lower: They symbolise a person's children, brothers and sisters.

Loose Teeth: Loose teeth implies that one of his family members will fall ill.

Teeth in the Pocket: Pocketing the teeth or wrapping them in cloth or seeing them falling into the hand or keeping them in the house _ any of these is a harbinger of a child, brother or sister being born. It may also mean his deriving some benefit from one of them.

Masticating Teeth: To see the teeth in the act of chewing suggest that one his family members will fall ill.

Long Teeth: If a person sees his teeth as long or white or beautiful, it means that he will witness certain conditions in some of his family members that will give him pleasure and satisfaction.

Molars: They symbolises a person's paternal uncles, aunts, etc. Any defect in them is suggestive of similar misfortune regarding them.

Canine: This symbolises the head of the household on whom the household depends.

Pre-molars: These symbolise one's maternal uncles and aunts.

Molars and Pre-molars: These symbolise a persons paternal and maternal uncles and aunts. The upper ones will then symbolise the males and the lower ones the females. If a person sees any of these as fallen, and he does not pick them up nor or count them, it means one of his relatives will die. And if he sees all of them, having fallen and he does not pick them up nor does he count them it suggests that he will outlive all of them, being the last to die.

An Incident: It is related that Ameerul-Mu'mineen, Mansoor, dreamt that he had lost all his teeth. In the morning he called for an interpreter. The interpreter came and after listening to the dream, said to Mansoor: "All your relatives will die." Upon this, Mansoor became infuriated, saying: "May Allah lock your mouth! May He never let your interpretation become a reality! Now be gone!". Then another interpreter was called who fortunately was familiar with courtly protocols. He said: "O Ameerul-Mu'mineen, you will live for a long time. You will be the last to die amongst your relatives."

Highly delighted with his tactful interpretation, the Ameerul-Mu'mineen laughed, remarking: "Both interpretations are the same, but the manner employed by you is more superior and excellent!" He then presented him ten thousand Dihrams as gift.

Neck: A long neck symbolises trust (*amaanat*) and Deen of Islam and the upholding of these two. A short neck will naturally imply a person's weakness and inability in upholding them.

The Brain: It symbolises people who are trustworthy.

The Hand and Arms: Both symbolise either the observer or his brother or companion - depending on which of the three is implicated in the dreams.

An Amputated Hand: If a person sees his hand being amputated, it suggests that either his brother of his friend will die; or his partner will dissolve his partnership wit the observer. The above will only true if the observer did not pick up the amputated limb. But if he did, it suggests that a brother or child will be born or he will befriend someone.

A Detached Hand with No Bleeding: If a person sees his hand as detached without any trace of blood it a glad tiding of the observer's abstinence from sins. The same is the interpretation if a person sees himself holding his neck with both hands.

The Hand Amputated by the King: If a person sees his hand being amputated by a king, it suggests that he will swear a false oath.

Long Arm: A long arm suggests increase in income and also excessive spending due to generosity.

Powerful Hands: Powerful hands symbolise the wielding of great power.

Fingers: They symbolise his brother's and sister's children (ie. nephews and nieces). At other times they symbolise the five daily salaah. Thus, if any defects are seen in a person's fingers, it is suggestive of similar shortcomings in his salaah; or it forewarns mishaps regarding his nephews or nieces _ depending entirely on which of the two aspects are implicated in the dream.

Nails: They symbolise a person's ability, capability and position _ since he uses his finger-nails to scratch his body.

Bosom: It symbolises a person's patience and tolerance. A wide bosom symbolises great tolerance while a small one bespeaks of little or no tolerance at all.

Breasts: These symbolises a person's daughters.

Stomach: It symbolises a person's assets and his sons. To see one's stomach smaller than its normal size suggests that his wealth will increase.

The Stomach, Intestines and Other Organs: The stomach, intestines etc. symbolise a person's hidden wealth which he had accumulated over the years.

Eating One's Intestines, Liver and Kidney: If a person sees himself eating his own intestines, liver or kidneys or any other organ situated in or around the stomach it means he will have access to all his wealth which was not available to him hitherto. The same is the interpretation if _ instead of eating them _ he sees himself or another picking them up or carrying them.

Parasites: Any parasite whose life depends on the human body symbolises a person sees stomach-worms and lice walking on his body in great numbers or he sees them walking on his clothes it suggests that he will acquire much wealth and many male children.

The Ribs: The ribs symbolise the women of his household. Any pain in the ribs is suggestive of similar mishaps in them.

The Back and Loins: These symbolise a person's honour, dignity and nobility. At other times the back or the loins symbolise a child since a child is born of a person's back.

The Shoulder: It symbolises a person's wife. Any defect seen in the shoulder is suggestive of similar mishaps regarding his wife.

The Male Generative Organ: if cut it means either he or his son will die. If he sees more than one it means the same number of children will be born to him.

The Testicles: They symbolise his daughters. Any pleasant or unpleasant occurrence in them bespeaks of similar pleasant or unpleasant occurrence in his daughters.

The Left Testicle: The left testicle means a son will be born to him. If the left one is ripped or missing, it means no sons will be born to him.

The Thighs: To see one's thigh amputated or detached from the body means that one will separate from his family members.

The Knee: The knee, shin and feet symbolise wealth belonging to others. The same represents his livelihood on which he is dependent.

The Toes: They symbolise the beautiful image portrayed by what a man owns.

Tendons and Muscles: They represent all that links a man with his affairs, honour and dignity.

The Skin: It represents a man's estates after he dies.

The Portions Between the Navel and Knees: If any portion between the navel and knees is seen as exposed, it means a person's secrets will be divulged to the people. How much will be divulged depends on how much of that portion is exposed.

Nakedness: Stark nakedness means that the person will soon cease to seek his pursuit or it means that the present phase will soon pass. But, it the observer of such a dream is a person whose pursuit is Deen, he will attain high status in piety, adoration, obedience and devotion to Allah. And if his pursuit is material wealth then he will attain this to the extremes provided none had seen his *aurah* (ie. any portion between the navel and the knees). On the contrary if his *aurah* becomes exposed to people, then nothing good is to be expected of such a dream.

Nudity in the Masjid: If a person sees himself as nude in the masjid or market place or in any other place, provided non had seen his *aurah* nor had anyone taunted him it suggests cheerfulness after sorrow, good health after sickness, atonement from sins and freedom from debts.

The Neck: If the neck is severed from the body it means that the person will become free if he is a slave or he will recover from his illness or he will soon be freed of his debts.

The same dream could also be interpreted as follows: he will proceed for Hajj; or if he is distressed, he will soon find relief; or if he is in fear, it will e removed.

Bleeding: If a person sees himself as a mediator between two groups of people it means he will reach some agreement with his opposition provided the person acting as the mediator does not see blood oozing from his body. Otherwise there is no good to be expected. The same dream could also mean that there is doubt insofar as the lawfulness of his wealth is concerned.

Slaughtering a Man: This indicates that the slaughterer will subject the man to oppression, for slaughtering something that is not edible is oppression.

Slaughtering a Haraam Animal: This means he will oppress someone whom the Haraam animal represents.

Killing a Person: This means that the victim will acquire some good from the killer in real life.

Wrestling with a Person: The person who loses the duel in the dream will gain victory and live prosperously in real life. It could also mean that the loser will gain more land than the winner.

Abusive Language: Abusing and swearing someone means that the abused person is on a better footing than the abuser.

An Incident: It is related that Abdullah bin Zubair ؓ saw in his dram that he is engaged in a duel with Abdul Malik ibn Marwan defeating the latter. The former also sees himself pinning his foe to the ground by means of four nails. When he awoke in the morning, he sent his man to Muhammad bin Sireen ؒ for the interpretation of the dream. He also cautioned him not to reveal to the Imaam the name of the one who saw the dream, nor the winner nor the loser. When the Imaam heard this he exclaimed: "This is not your dream! Nor can anyone except Abdul Malik ibn Marwan or Abdullah bin Zubair see such a dream!" The person insisted that it was he who had seen the dream. The Imaam declined to interpret the dream. The person returned to Abdullah bin Zubair and informed him of the Imaam's refusal to interpret the dream until the real person who had seen the dream is not known. Abdullah bin Zubair ؓ sent his messenger back to tell the Imaam that it was he who had seen the dream. When the Imaam was informed of this and the fact that the loser was Abdul Malik bin Marwan he said that Ibne Marwan will gain victory over Abdullah bin Zubair, killing him in the process. Thereafter, the chain of Khilafat will remain in the family of Ibne Marwan. This interpretation was given because of the fact that Ibne Marwan was pinned to the ground by means of four nails. The interpretation turned out to be exactly as the Imaam had stated!

Bridegroom: If a person sees himself as having become a bridegroom and he also recognises his bride in the dream it is a glad tiding that he will soon marry, or he will wield power or he will become the owner of something of value. But if he did not see his bride nor does he see himself in wedlock with a woman it means that he will either die or be killed or become a martyr.

Divorce: Divorcing one's wife means that the person will be dismissed from his present position.

Blood, Pus etc. without any Wound: Bleeding without any wound means he will acquire unlawful wealth. Similarly, pus or blood gushing forth from a fountain in the body and such pus or blood staining his body also means he will earn haraam wealth. How much haraam wealth he earns depends on how much blood or pus gushes from such a fountain. But if the body does not stain it means he will be demoted from his present position. The degree of his demotion depends on how much blood or pus gushes out.

Wounds, Bruises etc.: Wounds, bruises, ulcers, sores etc. appearing on the body symbolise wealth that will be acquired by the observer of such a dream. The extent of the wealth will depend on how old such wounds, bruises etc. are. Likewise, any obesity or swelling means acquiring of wealth equal to the extent of the obesity or size of the swelling.

Leprosy: It symbolises the acquisition of abundant and pure wealth.

Insanity: It symbolises wealth except that the person will spend it in an undesirable manner and in evil places.

Intoxication: It symbolises wealth which will be acquired from a king if such intoxication is caused by wine. If not, then no goodness is to be expected from such a dream.

Emaciation and Weakness: Thinness and weakness of the body denotes that not much good is to be expected from such a dream.

Power: Power in the dream signifies strength in one's Deen and position.

Carrying a Burden: Carrying a burden signifies that the person will soon be faced with grief and sorrow.

Excreta of Man and Animals: This symbolises wealth. If it gives off a bad smell it symbolises unlawful wealth. The stronger the odour the greater the unlawfulness.

Droppings of Animals that are not Eaten: It symbolises haraam wealth.

Becoming Spattered with Excreta: If a person sees himself or his clothes spattered with excreta of animals which are haraam to consume or he becomes the owner of the excreta or he sees himself guarding such excreta, it means he will receive unlawful wealth.

Passing of Stools: Seeing oneself passing stools means he will lose wealth equal to the extent of stools passed. Or he will conduct himself in such a manner as will cause him harm. If so much stools are passed that it takes the form of mud, rain or floods then there is no good to be expected from such a dream. Perhaps it could mean he will be terrorised by the authorities.

Passing of Anything besides Stools: The passing of anything unusual such as blood, worms, lice, pus etc. denotes that the observer of the dream will suffer loss in his wealth and family accordingly.

Breaking Wind: If it is with sound, it means he will utter such words as will make people laugh.

Bleeding from the Anus: If a person sees himself bleeding from the back passage and his body becomes stained with such bleeding, it means he will acquire wealth equal to how much his body is stained.

Spitting: This means he will utter words which will affect someone other than himself.

Coughing: Coughing means that the person will complain about someone.

Blowing the Nose: Blowing the nose and expelling filth mens that the person will become angry as a result of which he will utter undesirable words. If now filth is expelled it means he will lodge a complaint against someone.

Vomiting: Vomiting without an unpleasant odour, taste and colour is a glad tiding that the person will cease to commit sins and that he will resort to sincere repentance. But if has an unpleasant odour, taste or colour, he will commit an evil act which will prove to be detrimental to him.

Cupping: If the cupper is unknown it means that he will be subjected to a condition or he will be made to guard a trust. But if the cupper is a known person it means he will lose a portion of his wealth or belongings.

Cupping on the Neck: Either he will commit breach of trust or breach of trust will be committed in his property.

Bleeding from the Nose: A sign of good health. At times it indicates financial loss or dishonour or loss of one's capital.

Drawing Blood from the Vein: It implies a person losing part of his wealth to the king or authorities.

Blood in a Cup, Bowl or Tray: This symbolises sickness and the spending of one's wealth on some woman. Some say spending it on oneself.

To be Stained with Blood, Dung etc.: If the body is seen stained with blood, dung, excreta and all that issue from the body, it symbolises unlawful wealth owned by him or it means he will receive haraam wealth in the future.

Incident 1: A person approached Imaam Muhammad bin Sireen ﷺ and said: "I have seen a dream that I have shaven my hair" or he said "I have seen my head shaven. Please interpret the dream for me". The Imaam said: "This slave of yours will be separated from you either by becoming free or by your death or his."(The narrator says) that the master died within five or six days after seeing this dream.

Incident 2: It is narrated that a person came to Imaam Ja'far Saadiq ﷺ and said: "I dreamed that a woman shaved my beard and hair. What is the interpretation? He said: "Indeed, you have seen a most unpleasant dream. For the woman symbolises the year (time) and the head symbolises a man's honour, respect, beauty and all that Allah favours him with. You will lose all of these. But since you have seen a woman do this, all these bounties will be recovered shortly." (The narrator says that) the dream came true after a short period of time.

Incident 3: It is related that in Baghdad some persons were seated together, relating their dreams to each other. One amongst them said: "Friends, I wish to relate to you a strange dream I had seen. I saw a barber shaving off my beard and moustache. On awakening I proceeded to Imaam Ja'far Saadiq ﷺ and related to him the dream. He said: *You are to become embroiled in some difficulty owing to which you will lose your honour and respectability amongst the people. This will cause you much grief and sorrow.* I was shocked by this interpretation. I returned home with difficulty and remained indoors for four days. On the fifth day I decided to go out for a walk. When I reached the door of the masjid, I saw an old acquaintance of mine being led out of the jail. The jailers then began taking of his clothes in order to lash him. Suddenly his gaze fell on me and he began crying out: *Hey So-and-so!* I responded: *I am present!* He said: *It is through you that I have landed in this misery. Hey So-and-so! whatever I have given you which you had carried to your house, return it to its owner and free me from this misery!* I said to him: *I seek Allah's protection from the accursed devil! For Allah's sake! you have given me nothing at all and what you are accusing me of, is all a lie!* He again said: *For Allah's sake, don't become difficult! I have given you such and such clothing belonging to so-and-so and you have hidden it in your house!*

"Hearing all this the police arrested me straight away and put me behind bars. They began interrogating me about something that I had never done. After some days I was brought before the Qaadhi to face the charges brought against me. I was found guilty and awarded the penalty for theft.

"I became popular in the whole of Baghdaad as an accomplice of thieves. But Allah's bounties know no bounds. A few days before my hand was to be amputated, a son was born to the Khaleefah. In jubilation, he decided to release all prisoners amongst whom I was one. I thanked Allah a thousand times for favouring me with His special bounty. This is how my dream became a reality. I have never seen a dream come out so true as this one."

Incident 4: A person approached Imaam Muhammad bin Sireen ﷺ and revealed the following dream: "I saw a black, stout woman in my dream whom I asked to marry me. Please tell me what is the interpretation?" The Imaam asked: "Do you know this woman?" He replied: "Ye". The Imaam said: "Then why the delay in works of piety? Proceed straightaway and get married to her. For her black colour suggests that she is well to do. And her height suggests that she will not live long."

Hearing this, the person approached the woman, proposed marriage to her and subsequently married her. Not many days passed before she suddenly died and he became her only heir to all her wealth. In this way the Imaam's interpretation became a reality.

Incident 5: A person narrated the following dream to Imaam Muhammad bin Sireen: "I saw in the dream that my son bound my hands behind my back with a black rope. Tell me what does this mean." The Imaam said: " Congratulations to you. You are in debt and your son will relieve you of this burden very shortly. Moreover, he will also relieve you of your burden of having to earn a livelihood and incurring further debts. For, blackness suggests affluence and sufficiency". This person thanked the Imaam saying: "My master, you have spoken the truth."

Section 10 :

Dreaming of Weddings, Female Generative Organs, Pregnancy, Deliveries, Breast-feeding etc.

Wedding: A wedding symbolises the acquiring of honour, dignity, pomp and material wealth, its measure depending on the beauty, pedigree and social status of his bride in the dream.

Marrying a Dead Woman: He will succeed in acquiring his pursuit regarding which he has lost all hopes.

Seminal Discharge: If a person dreams that he had emitted semen without having had intercourse and without having seen a woman in his dream it means he will become a mean of killing someone.

Greeting with *Salaam*: Saying salaam to a known person means marriage will be proposed to such a person for oneself, one's son or another party. If the other person responds to the *salaam*, it means the proposal will be accepted. Otherwise, not. But if he not known to him it means that he may get married in a foreign land.

Marriage of a Wife: If a person sees his wife getting married to someone else, it means her household will become wealthy and prosperous.

Marriage to One's Mother, Sister etc.: If a person dreams that he is marrying his mother, sister or any such person with whom marriage is forbidden in Islam _ and such a dream is seen in any of the sacred months of Thil-Qa'dah, Thil-Hijjah, Muharram or Rajab _ it means he will proceed to Makkah and Madeenah. But if such a dream is not seen in any of the said months it means he will treat his relatives with kindness and serve them well. If his relationship with them was estranged, it will be re-established.

Marriage of a Man to a Man: If a person sees himself marrying an unknown young man, it means he will gain victory over his enemy. But if he is known and there is no enmity between them then he the "bride" will acquire some goodness from either the "groom" or someone who resembles him in name or personality.

A Woman with Male Generative Organ: If a person sees a woman with a male generative organ it means she will give birth to a son if she is pregnant in real life. Moreover, the son will grow up with good character and leadership qualities. But if she is not expecting in reality, and she already has a child it means that whenever she does give birth she will do so to a son whose up bringing will be as mentioned above.

A Woman with a Beard: This may be a reference to her husband who will enjoy a good reputation as a result of his high standing in the community.

A Man with a Pudenda: The Arabic word for *pudenda* is *farj* which connotes openness, vastness, ease, comfort, luxury, joy and relief after sorrow. Thus, if a man sees himself with one it means comfort, affluence and joy after sorrow.

If he sees himself being copulated in the pudenda by some known person it means his needs will be fulfilled by that person but after much humiliation. And if the person is not known to him it suggests humiliation and disgrace.

Menstruation: If a person sees his wife menstruating it means his work will be obstructed. If he sees himself as menstruating he will commit evil.

State of Impurity: If he sees himself in the state of impurity (needing ghusl) his affairs will be jumbled.

Any dream that causes seminal emission whereby ghusl becomes necessary, such a dream has no interpretation. For, nocturnal emission is a result of the one's evil thoughts and the promptings of the cursed Shaytaan.

A True Incident: Imaam Muhammad bin Sireen رحمة الله عليه was approached by a person who said that he saw a very shameful and disturbing dream and that he was ashamed to reveal it because of its nature. The Imaam asked him to write down the dream on a sheet of paper. He wrote that he had been away from home for three months. During his absence he dreamed that he has returned home, finding his wife asleep on her bed while two sheep with horns were engaged in battle near her bed. The one injured the other. Because of this dream he has avoided approaching his wife and yet, by Allah, he loved her a great deal.

When the Imaam read this letter, he said to him not to leave his wife as she was a chaste and honourable woman. He explained the dream thus: "When she heard that you were returning home shortly, in fact you were almost home, she urgently sought for something with which to remove her pubic hair. Finding nothing she chose to use a scissors rather. In her haste, she injured herself causing a deep wound on that part of her body. To confirm this, go straight to her and see for yourself."

The man went straight to his wife expressing his desire to fulfil his need. She said: "No! not until you explain to me why you had avoided me for seven months!" He gave his explanation regarding his dream and the interpretation given by the learned Imaam. Upon this she exclaimed: "The Imaam has spoken the truth!" Then she took his hand and passed it over the cotton wool covering the sound. When he was satisfied he went back to the Imaam to report his findings. The Imaam praised and glorified Allah for having guided him to the correct interpretation of the dream.

Pregnancy: This symbolises a person's increment in material wealth. At times it represents fear for a certain person in view of the following adage: *Qad habala fil ardhi khawfu fulaanin.* This means that the earth is pregnant and burdened as a result of terror caused by so-and-so.

Delivering a Female Issue: If a person sees a daughter born to him it means he will soon find relief from his difficulties and he will receive plentiful sustenance. The same applies to purchasing a female slave.

Delivering a Male Issue: If a son is born to him, it means he will soon be faced with difficulties, hardships and anxiety. The same applies to buying a male slave.

Delivery by an Expectant Wife: If a person sees his wife giving birth to a boy whilst she is expecting in real life, she will give birth to a girl. And if she gives birth to a girl, she will deliver a boy.

Beast Feeding: If a person sees himself breast feeding or being breast fed, he will soon be imprisoned and the prison doors will be closed on him for a long time.

And Allah knows best.

Section 11 :

Dreaming of Death, Dead Persons, and Reports given by them

Death: Death in the dream symbolises corruption of a person's Deen while there will be glory, rank and honour for him in the world if such death is not accompanied by mourning, weeping, the carrying of a bier or corpse or the act of burying.

If the corpse is seen as buried, it means there is no more hope for the improvement of his Deeni matters: the devil will take charge of his life and he will be overwhelmed by the quest of material wealth. Also the same number of people will be influenced by the dreamer whose numbers he had seen following his bier. He will dominate and subjugate them.

On the contrary, if death is not accompanied by anything that suggests burial, mourning, weeping, giving of *ghusl, takfeen,* the carrying of the bier or corpse, it may mean that a portion of his house will be destroyed, or its wall or its timber will fall down. Some interpreters have said that perhaps he will weaken in the matter of his Deen and he will lose his insight and prudence.

Alive in the Grave: If a person sees himself as alive in the grave he will either be imprisoned or he will find himself in some straitened circumstances.

Digging One's Own Grave: Seeing oneself digging one's own grave means one will build or oneself a house in that town or place.

Speaking to the Dead: If a person sees himself as asking a dead person about anything regarding the dead person's or another's condition then the answer of the dead person will be true to its word _ whether good or bad _ for the dead person dwells in the world of truthfulness (ie. aakhirah) as opposed to the world of falsehood (ie. dunya). Thus, he does not speak a lie in whatever report he gives.

Seeing a Deceased Person as Happy: Seeing a deceased person in a good condition such as donning white or green clothes while he is laughing or giving glad tidings means that he, the dead man is in peaceful and happy condition.

Seeing a Deceased Person as Unhappy: Seeing a dead person as dishevelled with dust on his body or donning old, torn and tattered clothes or as angry means that he is not in a peaceful condition in the hereafter.

To see him as ill means he is burdened with sins.

Dying for the Second Time: If a dead person is seen as dying again and there is weeping without screaming and mourning it means a relative of his will get married and the marriage will bring great happiness and pleasure.

But if there is screaming and mourning then it means a close family member will die.

Digging the grave of a Dead Person: If a person sees himself digging the grave of a dead person who is known to him it means he will follow in his footsteps in worldly as well as religious matters. If he is unknown to him, he will pursue a matter wherein he will not succeed.

An Incident: It is related that when Imaam Abu Haneefah رحمة الله عليه was still a child, he dreamed that he was digging the grave of Rasoolullah ﷺ. He related the dream to one of his tutors in the *maktab*. The teacher said to him: "My child, if your dream is genuine then you will follow in the footsteps of Rasoolullah ﷺ and you will also do great research in his *shari'ah*". Every word of the interpretation manifested itself to be true and correct as is known by one and all.

Accepting from or Giving to the Deceased Something: Accepting something from the dead is regarded as good while giving him something is regarded as bad.

If a person sees a dead person giving him something of his world it means he will acquire livelihood from an unimaginable source. And if he sees himself giving a dead person clothes normally worn by living persons and he accepts such clothes and wears them it means he (the giver) has a short life span.

Carrying the Dead: If a person sees himself carrying a dead person in any manner other than the normal manner of carrying a bier or corpse it means he will carry a burden of haraam wealth. Some interpreters say that the same dream could mean that his is spending his wealth on some pervert.

If a person sees himself as carrying a dead person in a normal way it means he will either obey and follow the ruler of the time or he will take upon himself some of his responsibilities.

Embracing a Dead Person: If a person sees a dead person embracing him, squeezing him or killing him it means he will attain a good old age.

Entering an Unknown House with the Dead: Entering an unknown house in the company of a dead person means he will die soon and thus join the dead person.

A Dead Person Entering the Home of a Sick Person: Either his sickness will prolong or he will die soon.

Giving the Dead *Roti*, Bread or a Ring: It means a son will be born to him and he will die; or if he is wealthy he will lose his wealth.

And Allah, The Pure and Sublime knows best.

Section 12 :

Seeing Clothes, Garments, Carpets etc. in One's Dream

Garments are interpreted according to their origin (ie. of what material thcy are made), type and kind (ie. of what quality they are).

Garments of Silk, Raw Silk and Fine Silk: These symbolise superiority, strength, influence and the acquiring of unlawful wealth.

Woollen Clothes: Donning of woollen clothes means acquiring of material wealth in abundance. Clothing made of hair (such as camel's) or cotton wool or just cotton means acquiring of wealth to a lesser degree.

Sheet Worn as a Garment: A sheet worn as a garment means the acquiring of the material world as well as Deen.

Shirt or *Kurtah*: A shirt or *kurtah* symbolises the Deeni and worldly life of the dreamer. The longer the shirt or *kurtah* the greater his involvement in Deen and worldly matters.

Old Clothes: Seeing old clothes means the viewer of such a dream has a short life span.

Soiled Clothes: Such a dream is not a good reflection on the Deeni and worldly life of a person.

Dirt and Filth: Filth on the head, hair or body symbolises grief and sorrow.

White and Clean Clothes: Donning white, clean clothes reflects a favourable condition of the person who wears them.

Clothes that are Joined: Joined clothes, if they are soiled, means the one who wear them will become poor and needy.

Patched Clothes: A heap or stack of patched clothes symbolises extreme poverty and indigence.

Embroidered Clothes: Wearing white embroidered clothes means the attainment of the world as well as Deen. Also power and fame.

Turban: A turban generally symbolises authority. The extent to which a turban is fastened around the head represents the extent to which a person would enjoy his authority. The longer his turban the greater his authority.

A Silk Turban: Wearing a turban made of silk or raw silk means a persons's authority will cause his downfall in matters pertaining to his Deen and world. Also, whatever his earns during his term of office will be unlawful.

A Woolen or Cotton Turban: Wearing a turban made of wool or cotton means the person will yield power of a profitable nature. It will profit him in both Deeni and worldly matters.

Headgear or *Topi*: A *topi* symbolises either a person's capital, his brother, his son or his leader. Any excellence or defect seen in a *topi* bespeaks of similar excellence or defect in any of the above. Thus, a hole or tearing reflects an evil plight or grief or sorrow for any of the above persons; perhaps his capital will be lost due to some unforeseen circumstances.

A Long Coat Such as An *Achkan* or *Jubbah*: This is a glad tiding of some happiness coming his way.

A Long Coat With a Lining: It represents a person's wife. Similarly a blanket, pyjamas and a sheet on which one sleeps. If any of the above is seen as burnt or snatched away from him it means he will separate from his wife either by way of a divorce or death.

If he is seen as being prevented from acquiring any of the above or if any of the above is seen as being stolen from him it means he will intend divorcing his wife but without success.

A Pair of Shoes: If both shoes are seen as torn so badly that they are completely ruined it means his wife will die.

A Shoe: Sometime one shoe symbolises his partner or brother. If this is seen as torn or cracked while he walks in the other it means he will separate from his partner, brother or sister.

Good Smelling Sock: It symbolises the security of his wealth. If they are without any defect, giving off a good odour, it means he will discharge Zakaah and his wealth will remain protected against all calamities. Also his wealth will be purified and his own condition will improve.

Torn Stocks: If the socks are seen as torn or part of it as ruined, it means he will not discharge his Zakaah nor will he give charity. We seek Allah's protection from this.

Leather Socks or *Khuff*: It symbolises the security of a person's livelihood. If they are not defective it means he will continue to receive lawful sustenance. At times it symbolises grief and sorrow as well.

Wearing Torn Garments: If a person wears torn clothes while he is mending them it means his financial condition will improve. Also he is to acquire adequate sustenance.

In all conditions, garments bespeak a person's condition (as understood from above). Similarly, if he is a sinner, his condition will improve through repentance.

A Wife's Garments: If a person sees himself as sewing or joining his wife's garments or *burqa* or head-cloth, it means he will quarrel with her and she is turn will come to find out all that his relatives know.

Head-cloth or *Odhni*: A wife's head-cloth (ie. *odhni*, scarf etc.), *izaar*, or *burqa* represents her husband. Any excellence or defect seen in any of the above is a reflection of a similar excellence or defect in her husband.

A Spinning Wheel: A spinning wheel used for separating the seed from cotton symbolises a journey to be undertaken.

If a man sees himself as spinning wool, hair or camel hair it means he will soon undertake a journey and return with *halaal* provision in abundance and wealth which will be a means of great *barakah* and blessings for him.

If he sees himself as spinning cotton or the bark of tree such as is normally done by women it means he will undertake a journey and will return with goods. But such goods will be regarded as undesirable or unclean by the people.

If a woman happens to see the same dream it means that her relative who is absent will return soon.

A Woman Acquiring a Spinning Wheel: If a woman dreams that she has acquired a spinning wheel, if she is expecting, she will give birth to a girl. Otherwise a sister will be born. If such a spinning wheel has a spindle or rod, It means she will get her daughter married.

A Wife Donning the Clothes of her husband: This is a good and pleasant dream.

A Wife Wearing the Military Clothes of her Husband: The interpretation of such a dream is linked with either her husband or one who guard her.

The same dream could mean that either she will benefit from the good qualities of her husband or he will benefit from her good qualities.

Donning Feminine Clothes: If a man sees himself as donning feminine clothes it means he will experience tremendous fear, destitution and helplessness after which it will disappear by the will of Allah Ta'ala.

Donning Clothes of Various Colours: He will soon learn about the unpleasant things said about him. He will also be overwhelmed with fear. As a result of this he will become popular amongst the people.

Donning White Clothes: A very pleasant dream suggesting goodness and success in all matters.

Donning Yellow Clothes: It suggests sickness and anxiety. But there is no harm if this colour is seen in a long coat such as a *jubbah* or *achkan*.

Donning Green Clothes: A pleasant dream for both the living and dead since green is the colour of the people of Jannah.

Donning Red Clothes: Donning of red clothes is suggestive of a person's popularity.

Donning Black Clothes: If it is a person who is in the habit of wearing black clothes, it means he will acquire steadfastness, power, wealth and soundness in all his affairs.

Black Colour: Black colour in all things is regarded as good and pleasant except in grapes. There is no good to be expected in them.

Carpet or Mat : A carpet or mat symbolises the material things of this world and a person's age.

A Thick and Wide Carpet: A thick, wide and new carpet means he will live long, enjoy a peaceful life, receive ample sustenance and acquire much of the material things of this world.

A Thick but Narrow Carpet: It means a long life for him but not plentiful of sustenance.

A Thin but Wide Carpet: If the carpet is abnormally thin but wide it means plentiful of *rizq* but a short span of life.

A Thin, Old, Torn and Short Carpet: It is a bad omen. There is no goodness to be found in such a dream. The same is the case with a carpet that is folded or rolled up.

A Handkerchief: A handkerchief, towel or pillow represents a person's servants and subordinates. Any defects in any of the above bespeaks of similar defects in them.

Curtains: They symbolise grief, sorrow and anxiety for the one who sees them. No goodness is to be found in such a dream whether the curtains are new or old, few or many.

And Allah knows best.

Section 13 :

Dreaming of Jewellry, Gold, Silver, Coins etc.

Jewellry: It its quantity is known it symbolises women, children and servants. If it is so much that its quantity is not known it symbolises the Holy Qur'an, religious knowledge, *tasbeeh* and *thikr* of Allah Ta'ala.

Acquiring a Pearl: If a person sees himself as having acquired a pearl it means he will acquire a woman, slave-girl or servant.

Acquiring an Emerald or Ruby: If a person sees himself as having acquired an emerald or a ruby, if his wife is expecting, it means she will give birth to a girl.

Wearing a Pearl Necklace: If a person sees himself wearing a necklace made of pearls, it means he will commit the Holy Qur'aan to memory and he will become trustworthy and Allah fearing. He will be a person with a huge family. He will be held in high esteem by men and women alike. The more strings there are to such a necklace the greater will be his trustworthiness and esteem and family.

A Burdensome Necklace: If a person sees himself as being helpless in lifting a necklace and wearing it, it means he is a man of great Islamic learning but unable to act upon it.

Earrings: If a person sees himself as wearing earrings it means he will commit to memory the Holy Qur'aan, acquire Islamic knowledge and learn such *ilm* through which he will become a celebrity amongst the people.

For a woman, the mere seeing of earrings represent her husband and children.

Pearls Emanating from the Mouth: If a person sees pearls coming out from his mouth it means he will utter words of wisdom and piety. He will also disseminate the knowledge of the Holy Qur'aan and chant the praises of Allah Ta'ala.

Eating Pearls: If a person sees himself as eating or keeping pearls in his mouth, it means he will conceal the knowledge of Deen thereby depriving the people from benefiting from his *ilm*. At times eating pearls could mean reciting the Qur'aan and deriving benefit therefrom.

Scattering Pearls on the Road or in the Market Place: If a person sees himself scattering pearls on the road, in a garbage or in the market place it means he will acquire knowledge and wisdom and will teach it to unworthy people.

A Silver or Gold Necklace Studded with Jewels: Seeing the above in the dream means that a person will be made to guard some trust.

At times jewels, if mined and their quantity is not known, mean fortunes from which a person will derive much benefit.

Shells: They symbolise wealth of little or no benefit at all. At times they symbolise knowledge of no benefit. If they are few, it may symbolise women and servants.

Jewellry: Jewellry normally worn by men symbolises beauty and adornment. The more beautiful such jewellry the greater the beauty and adornment.

A Waist-band: A waist-band, if gilded, means the acquiring of wealth and the commanding of respect which will be a means of a person becoming boastful. It is also interpreted as him becoming a leader of his community which he will enjoy for duration of half his life. And if it is gilded and adorned with pearls studded therein, he will become very wealthy due to which he will become the leader of his household; or a son will be born to him who will command much respect.

A Broken Waist-band: If a person sees his waist-band as broken, snatched or altered in any way, it means harm coming his way.

Crown: If a man sees a crown in his dream it means he will enjoy honour, dignity, power and sublimity in the world and not in the hereafter. Wearing a crown made of gold, silver or pearls means great resources as well as honour but disaster for one's Deen.

A Crown Seen by a Woman: If a woman sees a crown in her dream, it symbolises her husband. If she is unmarried, she will soon marry a very dignified, respectable and influential man.

Pillory: A pillory of chain around the neck means a person will soon be given a trust to look after.

A Ring: A ring in the dream symbolises a person's estate, wealth, honour and power through which he enjoys a status and dignity amongst the people. Any abnormalities or excellences in the ring is a reflection of similar abnormalities or excellences in any of the above.

Acquiring a Ring: If a person sees himself as being given a ring, he will receive land, property or wealth. At times a ring could be interpreted as a woman, child, animal and the like _ depending on the condition of the one who sees such a dream. Thus, if a king sees such a dream it would mean the extension of his empire. If a businessman or trader sees it, it would mean expansion in business.

Snatching a Ring: If a person sees his ring being snatched from his hand he will lose what he rightfully owns.

Theft of a Ring: If the ring is stolen or destroyed his business and livelihood will be disrupted. And he will find himself in straitened circumstances.

The Stone of a Ring: It symbolises beauty and adornment. If the ring is seen destroyed but not the stone, it means a person will lose what he owns but the people will continue to talk about its beauty.

It is also said that the stone of a ring symbolises a person's son through whom he will enjoy popularity amongst the people.

A Gold Ring: It symbolises unlawful and *haraam* wealth and clothing.

A Ring Made of Iron: Wealth that a person will receive from the king.

A Yellow Ring or a Ring Made of Lead: He will be the recipient of things of little value.

Wearing a Ring, Necklace or Earrings: If a person sees himself as wearing any of the above then there is some goodness to be found in such a dream though little.

Wearing Bracelets: If a person sees himself as wearing two bracelets, he will find himself in straitened circumstances and will face some unpleasant conditions.

Ankle-rings: If a person sees himself as having worn one or two ankle-rings, he will be faced with hardships, fear, imprisonment and the like.

Bracelet for the Upper Arm: It symbolises some unpleasant matter caused by his brother or friend. If it is made of silver the matter will be less unpleasant and it will disappear in a short period of time.

Jewellry Worn by Women: If they are made from gold or silver they symbolise a pleasant life and embellishment for the women. But if they are one or two ankle-rings or bracelets then they represent her husband, brother, or father. The same is the interpretation of a crown although according to some, it represents king or ruler.

Gold Coins: If the origin and quantity is unknown and they are more than four, its interpretation is somewhat unpleasant. It represents grief and sorrow which he will experience. Receiving any of these means his reputation will be harmed. This, in turn will lead to a dispute or quarrel. But if their quantity is known the matter will be less serious and it will be settled in due course.

A Single Gold Coin or Coins up to Four: They represent his children whose numbers depend on the numbers he had seen.

A Gold Coin without any Imprint: If this is seen in his dream a son will be born in his house.

Bars of Gold: Seeing bars of gold or crockery made from gold means losing some of a person's wealth or the king or governor becoming unhappy or disillusioned with him.

Coins of Silver: Their interpretation varies according to the nature of the people. If a person sees himself as receiving them in the dream it means he will receive them in real life. For some it could mean receiving sustenance after arguing and quarrelling. At other times it could mean exchange of good words.

Black Coins: Black coins that are counterfeit symbolise deception, lies and quarrelling.

Black Coins Contained in a Bag: If a person sees himself as receiving black coins contained in a bag or pocket, it means a secret will be told to him which he will guard as a trust to his utmost ability.

Giving Someone Black Coins: A secret will be divulged to him.

A Single Coin: It represents a young son. If it is stolen from him it means he will lose his son.

Coins Made from Copper, Bronze etc.: Receiving them symbolises evil gossiping about oneself and imprisonment. It could also mean unwholesome *rizq* and a lowly trade.

Bars of Silver: Seeing these in the dream is regarded as better than seeing bars of gold since they (bars of silver) symbolise excellence and good fortune. If a person sees himself as having received a piece of silver with no design on it, it means he will marry a beautiful woman.

Silver from its Mine: He will acquire a woman from an unimaginable place.

Bars of Iron, Steel or Lead: He will receive the fortunes of this world if they are in their original form or molten.

Smelting Gold, Silver etc.: If a person sees himself in the act of melting gold, silver, iron or lead and casting any of them into any form such as coins, it means he will become the subject of people's slandering and backbiting.

May Allah safeguard us against all calamities, hardships and suspicion. Ameen.

Section 14 :

Dreaming of Vessels, Vases, Utensils, Mirrors, Scissors etc.

Vessels symbolise servants and lads while stoves, hearths, grates, cauldrons, lamps, table-cloths etc. symbolise grief, sorrow and anxiety which will be felt by the head of the household if the Arabic masculine equivalent is used for any of the above words. But if it is used as a feminine such as *qidr, qifah, maa'idah, musarrajah* and *qas'ah*★, then they symbolise a person's wife. As for the word *sufrah* though feminine, it symbolises the husband all the same.

Whatever is made from copper or lead such as cups, saucers, plates, trays, kettles etc. they all symbolise a person's servants and lads.

Mirror: It symbolises a person's wife. If a person sees himself as looking into a mirror, if his wife is expecting, she will give birth to a son who will resemble him. But if she is not nor does he have a son it means he will lose his job and someone else will take his position.

If a pregnant woman sees herself looking into the mirror she will give birth to a girl who will resemble her in every way. But if she is not pregnant it means her husband will marry another woman who will occupy the same house.

If a little boy sees himself looking into a mirror, a brother resembling him will be born. And if a little girl happens to see the same dream her mother will give birth to a girl.

Needle: A needle symbolises an obedient wife.

Threading a Needle: Threading a needle as long as it is not used

---

★ *Qidr*: cauldron, cooking pot; *Qifah*: large basket; *Maa'idaah*: table-cloth; *Musarrajah*: lamp; *Qas'ah*: trough.

for sewing also symbolises a dutiful wife.

Threading and Sewing with a Needle: If a man sees himself as threading a needle and sewing the clothes of people it means he will counsel them. Some interpreters say it is message for him to reform and put right his affairs.

Sewing with a Threaded Needle: This means that his affairs will be se aright and he will attain respectability amongst the people.

Sewing the Clothes of One's Wife: If a person sees himself as sewing the clothes of his wife using needle and cotton then it is not regarded as a good dream. If the needle happens to break, his affairs will be disrupted and he will become needy and poor.

Comb: It means both happiness and ecstasy.

Combing the Hair and Beard: He grief and anxiety will disappear shortly. Some say it means goodness and happiness through beneficial knowledge. Likewise, people will also derive maximum benefit from his knowledge just as they do from a king, *mufti, doctor* or *khateeb*.

Scissors: If seen in the dream it denotes meeting someone.

Scissors Descending from the Sky: It denotes shortness of life for the person.

Clipping Hair or Wool with a Scissors: If a person sees himself cutting or clipping hair or wool using scissors it means he will amass great material wealth.

Glass: Anything made of glass such as tumbler or bottle symbolises household goods such as jar (for preserves), vessels of fine china, porcelain, chairs etc. It also symbolises male and female servants.

An Incident: A person revealed his dream to Imaam Muhammad bin Sireen ﷺ saying that he had seen a glass vessel in his hand. Suddenly it fell from his hand and broke. Or he said that he saw it broken in his hand while holding it. The Imaam asked whether his wife was expecting. When he said she was he said that she will die at the time of delivery and the boy will live. The interpretation materialised exactly as the Imaam had interpreted.

Section 15 :

Dreaming of Arms, Weapons etc.

Generally speaking, arms, firearms, ammunition and all other weapons _ primitive or modern _ symbolise power, strength, honour, superiority, victory and grandeur for the person who sees them in his dream. He will acquire these according to his intellect and popularity. Any modifications and improvements in them denote added honour, power and strength.

Theft or Destruction of a Weapon: If a person sees his weapon as stolen or snatched from him or broken ruined it denotes the weakening of his power and strength. The same is the case where the weapon is given away as a gift or sold thrown away or loaned to someone.

A Sword of Bow or Spear in the Hand: Armed with or using any of the above against someone means a person will soon wield power and strength.

Killing Someone Using a Sword: This is interpreted as quarrelling with that person and hurting his feelings through tongue lashing.

Striking Someone with a Spear: It symbolises his writings in books and Journals.

Injuring Someone with a Spear: It means the injured person will attain benefit through help and assistance.

Club: Striking someone with a club or walking stick or any weapon that is bent like a walking stick means that the victim will be involved in some difficulty that causes injury and damage.

Inflicting Injury: If injury is inflicted on someone, the injured person will be harmed by the one inflicting the injury and he will be humiliated to the extent of the wound.

Cutting a Limb: Cutting and separating someone's limb such as the head, hand, feet means a quarrel is imminent between the one who does this and the person whose limb had been cut. The same is the interpretation if his flesh is cut.

Receiving an Unsheathed Sword: If a person sees himself as receiving an unsheathed (naked) sword and he lifts it above his head but does not strike with it, it means he will wield such power as will make him popular; or he will father a very beautiful girl.

Regarding the above dream only Imaam Kirmani ﷻ says that a son or brother will be born in the home of the dreamer.

A Broken Sword in the Sheath: If a person dreams that a sword is given to him in its sheath and it breaks in the sheath it means his son will die while it is in its mother's womb.

A Sword in a Broken Sheath: If a person dreams that a sword is given to him in a broken sheath then the mother will die but his son will be saved.

A Sword with a Broken Handle: The father, paternal uncle or their equivalent will die.

A Sword with a Good or Defective Handle: Similar defect or good will become apparent in the father, uncle or their equivalent.

The Broken Point of a Sword: A person's mother, paternal grandmother, maternal aunt or some lady equal in status to any of these will die.

Wielding an Unsheathed Sword: Imaam Ja'far ﷻ says that anyone who sees himself as wielding a naked sword means he will speak out freely against the people and their affairs. And if he strikes someone with the sword but neither does he bleed nor the victim it means he will speak out openly against them. But if the victim bleeds in such a manner that the striker's body becomes soiled with his blood it means that in real life the victim will speak out freely against him or the striker will obtain unlawful wealth from him.

The Sword-belt Hanging from the Neck: If a person sees a sword-belt hanging from his neck in such a manner that the sword hangs on the ground, it means he will wield power proportionate to the length of the sword. But will at the same time be incapable of discharging his duties as a result of his weakness.

But if the sword is short (and it does not touch the ground) due to the shortness of the belt, it means he will relinquish his power due to his dislike for it.

If the belt is cut it means he will lose control of his power or be absolved from his duties.

A Painted Sword: If a person sees his sword painted, it means his words will hold no weight.

A Blunt Sword: No words will affect him in any way.

Spear: If other weapons are seen together with a spear it symbolises power and superiority and that his instructions will be carried out.

If no other weapons are seen with a spear then provided the spear has a point, a son or brother will be born in his home. And if it has no point then provided he is familiar with such a spear, only daughters will be born in his home. Seeing any excellence or defect in such a spear represents a similar excellence or defect in him.

A True Story: Abu Ammaarah Attayyaan رحمة الله reported to us that he revealed a dream of his to Imaam Muhammad bin Sireen رحمة الله that it was as if he had seen a spear or lance in his hand. The Imaam asked whether he had seen the point of the lance or not. He said no. Upon this he said: "Had you seen the point, a son would have been born to you. But now you will have female issues only." He pondered for a moment, then said: "In all, twelve daughters will be born to you."

(After many year) it is reported from Muhammad bin Yahya that when he revealed the above incident to Abul Waleed ﷺ, the latter laughed saying: "I am the son of one of them. I have eleven material aunts and Abu Ammaarah Attayyaan was my grandfather. May Allah shower His blessings upon him and us and all the Muslims."

A Bow and Arrow: A bow with an arrow about to be shot (but not shot) symbolises power and strength; or a son or brother will be born to him.

A Bow in its Cover: His wife is pregnant with a male issue in her stomach.

A Broken Bow: It is an omen that either he or his son or his brother will lose respectability and honour.

Discarding a Bow: If a person sees himself as throwing away his bow it means he will lose his respectability and honour. Some say he will undertake a journey and will return safely if the bowstring does not break. If it breaks he will remain at his destination.

Shooting with a Firearm: If a person sees himself as shooting someone with a firearm it means he will abuse and humiliate the person whom he shot.

Shooting an Arrow: Shooting an arrow means speaking out against evil. The extent to which the arrow penetrates decides the extent to which his words will have effect.

Shaping an Arrow: It symbolises honour and superiority. Or the birth of brother or son. Or marriage which will be a means of a son being born to him.

Confiscating a Bow from Another: If a person sees himself struggling with another in an effort to confiscate a bow from him but without success it means matters will become confusing and difficult for the person who is associated with such a bow. Such a person may be the king, a brother or son.

Armour, Helmet etc.: Armour coat of mail★, helmet, shield, flag etc, If seen in the dream means protection just as protection is sought through forts and shields. Also, victory, superiority and power will be acquired,

Shield: If seen together with a weapon it means protection against enemies. If seen alone it means he is an upright man who will afford protection to his brothers against evil and all sorts of harm.

Whip: A person will become a guardian to charitable trusts, small fortunes and the like.

★ A suit of armour made of linked material rings or overlapping plates.

Section 16 :

Seeing Horses, Mares, Mules, Donkeys etc. in One's Dream

Horse: A horse in the dream symbolises a person's status, rank, honour, dignity, power and glory. If he sees any increase in its quality and excellence it means similar increases in the quality an excellence of the above.

Mounting a Horse: If a person sees himself as mounting a horse which has no defects at all while such a horse trots slowly and gracefully, it means he will acquire honour, dignity and respectability. The same is the interpretation if he sees himself owning, acquiring or securing the horse. For Rasoolullah ﷺ has said: "Tie the horse. Surely, its back is a means of honour for you and its stomach a means of fortune".

Defective Saddle, Reins, Harness, Stirrup etc.: Any defect in any of the above means a person's honour and power will diminish according to the defect.

A Horse Having a Long or Short Tail: A hose with a long tall means a person will have many followers while a horse with a short or cut tail means he will have less followers.

Limbs of the Horse: Every limb of the horse represents a person's power and influence according to the importance of that limb.

A Fighting Horse: If a person sees the horse fighting with him it means he will commit a serious crime landing himself in some misfortune whose seriousness depends on the strength of such a horse.

An Uncontrollable Horse: If a horse is seen as going out of control in a confined area such as the top of a wall or roof or within the four walls of a masjid it means his honour and dignity will be tarnished. Perhaps he will commit a sin or crime of serious nature.

A Flying Horse: If a person sees himself as mounted on a horse which flies with him in the skies he will attain honour and dignity in both the worlds. Similar interpretation is given if he sees a horse with wings. It may also mean that its owner will undertake a journey soon.

Horse Running through Cities: If horses are seen running through cities or between houses it means floods, rains and disaster are imminent. But if such horses are seen with saddles it means the person seeing the dream will meet lots of people who will have gathered together for some happy or unhappy occasion.

A Spotted Horse: A spotted (white and black) horse means the owner will continue with the work he is doing for a long time or the matter with which he is linked will continue to persist.

A Black Horse: The owner will acquire abundant wealth and tremendous happiness.

A Reddish-blackish Horse: It denotes power and progress in Deen.

A Brown Horse: A brown or tawny-coloured horse means the owner will travel to some land where he will face hardships.

A White Horse: Conditions experienced by the owner will persist.

A Red Horse: It is best of all horses insofar as interpretation is concerned.

A Horse with White Feet: A horse with all its feet white is regarded as the most excellent amongst all houses.

Allowing Another Person to Ride With: If a person sees himself as allowing another person to ride with him on his horse it means he will have his mission accomplished through that person.

A Mare: A mare of female horse symbolises a woman. If a person sees himself as becoming the owner of a mare or as mounting his own mare it means he will acquire a good, honourable and blessed woman.

A Black Mare: He will marry a wealthy woman.

A White Mare with Black Spots: He will marry an exceptionally beautiful woman.

A Green Mare: He will marry a woman with a charming personality and a sweet, singing voice.

Theft of a Mare: If a person dreams his mare as being stolen or dead, the same will happen to his wife. If he sees any defect in her the same is to be expected with regards his wife.

Eating the Flesh of his Mare: Eating the Flesh of his mare means prosperity and honour. Also, he will enjoy a good reputation and receive subsistence (*rizq*).

An Unknown Horse: Seeing an unfamiliar horse which he does not own nor mounts means that he is a man of good repute and high honour. If he sees such a horse entering his neighbourhood or house it means a powerful and honourable person will make his appearance in that neighbourhood or house. If he sees such a horse leaving such a neighbourhood or house it, means a man with the same qualities mentioned above will leave the neighbourhood or house either by way of going away for good or death.

A Pack-horse: A horse meant for carrying burden symbolises a person's fortune and luck.

An Obedient Pack-horse: If such a horse is seen as well-trained and obedient it means good fate awaits him and if it is not seen as obedient then ill fate awaits him.

Mounting a Pack-horse: If he sees himself as mounting a pack-horse while he is in the habit of mounting an Arab horse it means his status will decrease and his happiness will come to an end. But if his habit *is* to mount such a horse his status will increase and he will become happy.

Mule: A mule symbolises a person who has no ancestral nobility yet possesses great physical strength and is of a temperamental disposition. Such a person may be a slave, shepherd or a person born out of wedlock.

Mounting a Mule: If a person who has an enemy with great physical strength, sees himself as mounting a mule then he (the observer of the dream) will overpower and gain victory over him. If a woman happens to see the same dream she will marry a man with great physical strength and of a temperamental disposition.

At times a mule is interpreted as a journey to be undertaken.

Mounting a She-mule: Mounting a she-mule which is well saddled and well-bridled symbolises a barren woman. The same is interpretation if ownership is taken to such a mule.

Mules of Various Colours: Their interpretation are exactly as the interpretations of horses of various colours.

Seeing a Female Mule: The mere seeing of a female mule in one's dream represents a person's honour, status, respectability and high standing in the community.

The Skin and Flesh of a Mule: They represent a person's wealth whose quantity equals the quantity of the skin and flesh seen in the dream.

The Milk of a Female Mule: The milk of a female mule does not augur well for the one who drinks it. Though he will receive some good he will experience much hardships depending on how much milk he had drunk.

An Ass: Seeing an as in the dream is regarded as better than seeing a pack-horse. It symbolises a person's good fortune and luck. Seeing any excellences or defects in an ass means similar excellences or defects in his luck.

The interpretation of a female ass is the same as a male ass.

Mounting an Ass: If a person sees himself as mounting an ass which is obedient, he will acquire abundant *rizq* and become prosperous.

A Black Ass: It means prosperity and becoming a leader in his community.

Donkeys of Various Colours: Their interpretations are exactly as the interpretations of horses of various colours.

The interpretation of mounting, securing, owning, surrounding and enclosing a donkey is the same as doing the same to a horse.

Falling from an Ass: If a person sees himself as mounting and riding as ass and then falling off it means his good condition will take a sudden turn for the worse. Perhaps he will die.

Dismounting an Ass: If a person sees himself as dismounting an ass in normal way then there is no harm in seeing such a dream.

Buying an Ass: If a person sees himself as buying a donkey, paying hard cash for it and handing such cash with his hands it means he will speak words of wisdom in the presence of people. And if he does not see himself as handling the cash although the price for the donkey is paid in full it means some good will come his way for which he will express his gratitude. For paying the price for anything is in reality expressing one's gratitude.

An Ass with Weak Eyesight: Seeing an as with weak eyesight means that matter relating to his livelihood will become confusing and difficult. The same applies to seeing an as which has only one eye.

A Disabled Ass: Seeing such an ass means he will not find proper guidelines regarding his mission.

An Ass Becoming a Mule: If a person sees his ass changing into a mule it means the fruits of his efforts will be enjoyed by an other. This will happen when he will be on a journey.

An Ass Becoming a Horse: This means he will receive his livelihood from a king or some dignified person.

A Weak Donkey: If a person sees his donkey as weak, unable to walk or carry a burden or walk uphill it means he will become unprosperous.

Eating the Flesh of an Ass: If he sees himself as eating the flesh of a donkey or taking possession of one or slaughtering it for food, it means he will receive unlawful wealth.

Drinking the Milk of a She-ass: It means severe illness with no hope of recovery.

And Allah Ta'ala knows best.

Section 17 :

Dreaming of Camels, Cows, Goats, Sheep, their Meats and Colours

Camel: A camel sometimes symbolises a journey, sometimes grief and at other times a huge and healthy person _ depending on circumstances. The same is the case when a strong, red camel is seen.

A She-camel: It represents a woman if the viewer of the dream is unmarried. Otherwise it means a journey, land, property or house.

Riding a Camel: Riding a camel means that a journey is to be undertaken.

Fighting a Camel: Fighting or quarrelling with a camel means he will fight with his enemy.

Driving a Herd of Camels: Driving a herd of camel or becoming the owner of such a herd means he will become the leader of a people.

An Unfamiliar Camel: If an unknown, ugly camel is seen appearing in an area or city or village it means either an enemy will make his appearance in that place or that place will be devastated by floods, plague or disease. But if the camel is seen as beautiful and healthy then the end result of the above calamities will be favourable and a means of blessings.

Camel Meat: It represents the belongings of the one who sees the dream.

Eating Camel Meat: It means illness for the one who eats it.

Milking a She-camel: The one who does this will acquire lawful wealth from a woman. But if, instead of milk, he takes out blood, puts or anything else from the udder the wealth thus acquired will be unlawful.

Drinking Camel Milk: Drinking camel milk without milking it means the person will acquire lawful wealth from someone who is physically strong, wields power and commands respect.

A Camel Calf that is Weaned: It symbolises a person's child.

A Camel that Escapes: An escaped, lost or stolen camel means that a person's wife will separate from him.

An Ox or Bull with Horns: It symbolises a big and powerful deputy of the king who wields great power and exercises great control. Such a person enjoys the liberty of granting benefits to others.

An Ox or Bull without Horns: It symbolises a mean, contemptible and short person who will be deprived of his wealth and natural talent or gift.

Mounting an Ox or Bull: Mounting an ox or becoming the owner of one means the person will be granted such a position by the king that other deputies of the king will be subservient to him. Moreover, by virtue of his status he will acquire good fortunes.

An Ox in the House: If an ox is seen entering his house and he ties it up in such a manner that it is under his control it means he will acquire wealth which he will guard closely. Thus, he will become prosperous.

Owning Many Oxen: He will become a manager of the financial affairs of a people.

Being Hit with the Horns of an Ox: He will be dismissed from his position and will suffer loss. And if the horns happen to break in the process he will face hardships in his work and his dismissal is imminent.

The Horns of an Ox: They represents a person's honour, dignity, respectability, wealth and weapons.

A Woman Mounting an Ox: If a woman sees herself as mounting an ox it means she will marry a man if she is unmarried. But if she is married her husband will obey her and she will take advantage of his good nature.

The Flesh of an Ox: It symbolises a person's wealth. And its skin represents his estate.

Slaughtering an Ox and Distributing its Meat: If a person sees himself slaughtering a working-ox (meant for ploughing), and distributing its meat it means he will die soon. But if it is not a working-ox he will die in the same place and his estates will be distributed.

A Calf: Slaughtering a calf or ox that has not yet worked in the fields means that the person will exploit another person, devouring his estates before his death.

A Herd of Oxen: Seeing a herd of oxen entering a locality or house while such oxen have no owners means that the people of that locality or house will be afflicted with some disease or plague. This is more true if the oxen are of variable colours or specially re or yellow.

A Cow: It symbolises the current year or a woman.

A Black Cow: It symblises a good and prosperous year.

A Herd of Black Cows: It symbolises many prosperous years depending on how fat they are.

Lean Cows: They symbolise drought and many lean years.

A Fat Cow: It symbolises a good and prosperous year if a person sees himself as becoming the owner of such a cow or if they belong to the people of that locality in which they are seen.

Beef: It symbolises wealth accumulated during those

prosperous years mentioned above. The same is the interpretation if the skin, urine, droppings or any other filth of the stomach is seen. But whether such wealth is lawful or unlawful will depend on the odour of the urine, droppings or filth.

The same interpretation will be given if, instead of cows, the urine, droppings etc. of other animals are seen.

If the odour is overpowering it represents wealth that is totally unlawful. There is no good to be expected from such wealth.

Ghee and Milk: They represent wealth and prosperity for the person who acquires or takes ownership of them.

Milking a Cow and Drinking its Milk: If a person sees himself milking an drinking cow milk it is a glad tiding that he will become rich; or if he is rich his wealth will increase; or if he is a slave he will become free and marry his mistress.

A Pregnant Cow: If this is seen in the dream then a prosperous year is to be expected. A year full of *barakah* and blessings. This is sure to happen.

Sheep: It symbolises a fit and healthy person who is known to the people. A person who is enviable _ one looked upon with respect. He is also an honourable, wealthy and brave person who takes special care in guarding himself in all respects.

Acquiring a Sheep: If a person sees himself acquiring or becoming the owner of a sheep it is glad tiding that he will acquire superiority and wealth. An influential and powerful person will become subservient to him.

Slaughtering a Sheep: If he sees himself as slaughtering or killing a sheep not for food it means he will subjugate or gain victory over a powerful and strong man.

Skinning a Sheep: In the above case if he sees himself as skinning the animal it means he will rob him of his wealth. He will enter into some dispute with him. Finally, he will separate from him.

Eating Mutton: In the above case if he sees himself as eating the meat of the animal it means he will usurp his wealth.

Mounting a Sheep: In the above case if he sees himself as riding the animal, leading it to wherever he desires it means he will derive tremendous benefit from such a person.

Carrying a Sheep on the Back: It means he will bear the expenses of another person.

A Sheep Mounting a Man: If a person sees a sheep mounting him and riding on him it means some powerful and strong man will subjugate him, rendering him powerless.

Overpowering a Sheep: In the above case if he sees himself as overpowering the sheep, dropping it to the ground, it means he will overpower him and render him helpless and powerless.

Becoming the Owner of a Flock of Sheep: If a person sees himself as becoming the owner of a flock of sheep it means he will gain superiority over some noblemen and great personalities. A similar interpretation is given if he sees himself as a shepherd of a flock of sheep.

Sacrificing a Sheep: If a person slaughters a sheep or any other animal with the objet of sacrifice or qurbani, it means he will be freed if he is a slave; or he will be released if he is imprisoned; or he will regain his strength and health if he is ill; or he will pay his debts if he is owing someone; or he will become wealthy if he is a destitute.

Ewe: It symbolises a noble, chaste and fortunate lady.

Acquiring an Ewe: Acquiring or becoming the owner of an ewe means he will acquire a woman with the above qualities.

Slaughtering an Ewe for its Meat: If a person sees himself as slaughtering an ewe for its meat, it is a glad tiding that he will receive some benefit from a woman.

Slaughtering an Ewe not for its Meat: It means he will marry a woman.

The Ewe Escaping: If he sees the ewe escaping from his house or dying or being stolen it means some unpleasant incident will be witnessed in his wife.

All Products of Sheep: The fat, meat, skin, milk, wool and droppings of sheep symbolise wealth and booty for a person if he sees himself as acquiring any of them.

A Lamb: It symbolises a child.

Receiving a Lamb as Gift: A child will be born to him.

Slaughtering a Lamb not for its Meat: A child or member of his family will die.

Eating the Meat of a Lamb: His child will become a means of prosperity for him.

Eating Half-cooked Meat of a Goat: He will become prosperous.

Eating the Raw Meat of a Goat: Eating raw meat of goat or striking someone with such meat means he will slander someone or speak ill behind his back.

Eating Roasted Meat: He will receive sustenance after much anxiety.

A Slaughtered and Skinned Goat Entering the House: If a person sees a slaughtered and skinned goat entering his house or any other place it means someone will die in that place.

A Limb of the Goat Skinned: If a limb of the goat is seen as skinned then that person towards whom the limb is linked will die.

Eating a Goat or its Limb: A child of his will die if eaten without cooking.

Eating the Flank or Ribs of a Goat: A woman will die in that place if its is eaten fresh, without cooking.

Becoming a Shepherd: If he sees himself as a shepherd, tending to goats, allowing them to graze, he will become the leader of his people or a ruler of the community.

Goat Hair: It is the same a s wool in all respects.

An Unknown Butcher: He represents the angle of death.

Buying Meat from the Butcher: If a person dreams that he has purchased meat from the butcher who delivers it to his house it means he will experience ailment in that portion of his body which is linked to the meat. If he pays for the meat it means he will be compensated for his difficulties. If not, he will not be compensated and will experience shock.

Becoming a Goat: If a person dreams that he is transformed into a goat, he will acquire blessings and piety.

The Liver, Fat, Spleen etc. of a Goat: The liver, fat, spleen, heart and kidneys of a goat symbolise a person's movable properties which he will remove or transfer from one place to another.

Eating the Innards of a Goat: If a person dreams that he is eating any portion of the innards (such as the liver, fat, spleen, heart etc.) of a goat, it means acquiring wealth. The same is the case if he becomes the owner of any portion of the innards. There is no difference as to whether they are cooked, roasted or fried. There is also no difference as to whether they are of a goat or any other animal. But the innards of a human being is regarded as more excellent.

Eating the Head of an Animal: This is a glad tiding that the one who eats this will be blessed with a long life and plentiful of wealth. And the head of a human being is regarded as better and more excellent.

And Allah knows best.

Section 18 :

Dreaming of Game and Other Wild Animals, their Meat and Milk

Wild Animals: If the males thereof are seen in the dream with no desire to hunt them, they represent such people who have no Deen; they have alienated themselves from the Muslim community so as to follow their own whims and fancies.

Mounting a Zebra: If a person sees himself as mounting a zebra or an antelope or a wild camel while he has no desire to hunt any of these, it means he will allow an evil person to enter his home, allowing him to do what he desires.

The same interpretation is given if, instead of mounting, he becomes the owner of any of the above animals or he subjugates them.

Hunting a Wild Animal: If a person sees himself as hunting a wild animal it means he will acquire wealth and booty _ whether the hunted animal is a male or female.

Hunting Wild Animals that are Females: They represent men, women and slave-girls.

Hunting a Female Gazelle or Buck: He will marry a beautiful woman.

A Wild Cow: It represents an exceptionally beautiful woman.

Killing a Wild Animal with No Purpose of Hunting: He will become a recipient of a fortune from some woman.

Rabbit: It represents a woman who is of no benefit or harm to a person.

The Young of Edible Game: They represent a person's children. Sometimes, slaves, if the person acquires any portion of their body.

Becoming the Owner of Wild Animals: If a person sees himself as becoming the owner of wild animals and these animals are under his full control so that he leads them to wherever he desires, it means, he will become the leader of a people.

The Skin etc. of Game: The skin, milk, fat etc. of game symbolise wealth and booty for a person if he sees himself as acquiring any of them.

And Allah Ta'ala knows best.

Section 19 :

Seeing Elephants and Beasts of Prey in the Dream

An elephant symbolises a foreigner who is despotic, powerful and vehement. He has no compassion _ striking fear into the hearts of people.

Mounting an Elephant: If a person sees himself as mounting or owning an elephant or encircling it or utilising it for any purpose other than ploughing, it is a glad tiding that he will either be endowed with power and superiority or he will be appointed to an important office by the government of a foreign country.

Eating Elephant Meat: The one who eats the meat will receive assets from some authority. The extent of such assets will depend on how much meat he eats. The same interpretation is given if a person sees himself taking possession of the skin, bone or any other portion of the elephant.

Riding an Elephant in Battle: He will gain victory over his enemy in battle.

A True Incident: This incident is related to a group of people living on the Island of Saqliyyah. It is narrated that their king was bent on annihilating the Muslims. For this, he prepared a powerful navy comprising of thousands of soldiers. At this point he saw a dream in which he saw himself mounted on an elephant while drums were beaten and trumpets were blown before him. When he awoke he summoned some of his clergymen and asked them to interpret the dream. They gave him the glad tiding of victory. He demanded proof from them for their interpretation. They said that the elephant is the most powerful animal on land and mounting such a powerful animal means becoming the master of power and strength. And the beating of drums and blowing of trumpets are signs of happiness, ecstasy and victory.˙ Also drums are only beaten in the presence of a king if there is some reason for happiness.

When the king heard this, he became both surprised and delighted. He then summoned some Jewish *ulama* and asked them for their interpretation. They also interpreted the dream as a glad tiding of victory. He then called some Muslim *ulama* and demanded that they interpret the dream. They all pointed to an experienced *aalim* to respond to the king's demand. The *aalim* said to the king that he would interpret the dream only if he guaranteed their safety which he did. The learned *aalim* interpreted the dream thus: "O king, I see no wisdom in your wanting to kill the Muslims and marching on them for this purpose. Please do not deploy your army for they will not return to you alive. They will be defeated and destroyed. And do not for one moment think that I give this interpretation because I am a Muslim". The king asked him for proof to which he replied that the Holy Book of Allah was the source for his proof. He quoted the verse: *Have you not seen what your Lord had done to the people of the elephants.* He recited the entire Soorah Feel. The king said: "This is your proof regarding the elephants. What have you to say about the drums?" He recited the verse: *And when the trumpet will be blown, this will be a very hard day for the non-believers _ not an easy one.*

When the king heard this he became utterly shocked and perplexed since the shaikh's explanation was rational and irrefutable. To avoid embarrassment to himself he dismissed the shaikh and his colleagues saying that he would have believed him if he (the shaikh) were not a Muslim. But since he is a Muslim he is based in his delivery of interpretation.

The shaikh said: "You will soon find out for yourself, o king!"

When the shaikh and his colleagues departed the king began to ponder deeply about what the shaikh had said. He became convinced and decided no to go ahead with his plans. When the clergy heard of this they approached him and urged him to ahead with his plan. They reasoned with him not to believe the interpretation of the shaikh as he was Muslim and a Muslim would obviously be opposed to killing Muslims. They also sought his permission to kill the shaikh which he refused. They continued to incite him against the Muslims and urged him to go ahead with his plans. He had no choice but to accede. He deployed a huge army under the command of his son. The two sides met in the middle of the sea. For three days a fierce battle ensued between the Muslims and non-Muslims. On the third day the Christians army was defeated. Not a single person was spared. When the king came to learn about this, he called for the shaikh and admitted his folly before him. He then secretly accepted Islam at his hands and bestowed many of his favours on him. It is said that he also learned the Holy Qur'an by the shaikh and his affair of the king became popular in Saqliyyah.

Lion: It symbolises a powerful and strong enemy. Fighting with a lion means one will soon fight an enemy that is strong and powerful.

Riding a Lion: Riding a lion and directing it to go wherever one please means one will soon be endowed with power and one's enemy will soon be subdued.

Facing a Lion: Facing or encountering a lion without becoming embroiled in a fight means a person will soon be terrorised by an authority or a powerful man. But no harm will come to him.

Eating Lion Meat: The one who eats the meat will receive riches from some authority or a powerful man.

The Skin of the Lion: It symbolises the estates and inheritance of some brave, dignified and powerful person.

A She-lion: Eating or acquiring the head of a she-lion means the acquiring of vast lands and estates.

Drinking the Milk of a Lioness: The person seeing this is to become prosperous. He will also overpower his enemy.

Tiger: It symbolises a powerful and dangerous enemy. Fighting with one means one will fight an enemy with great strength and power.

Riding a Tiger: One will attain dignity, honour and happiness. A strong and powerful opponent will be subdued.

Drinking Tiger Milk: It means profound grief and sorrow.

The Meat, Skin and Limbs of a Tiger: These are riches a person will acquire from some powerful enemy.

Panther: It represents a foolish friend and a person who has no knowledge of how to treat people according to their status.

Drinking the Milk of a Panther: The one who drinks the milk will attain much blessings and *barakah* in the near future.

Hyena: If a female, it represents an evil and ugly woman. If a male, it represents a disgraceful, cursed and contemptuous enemy.

Drinking Hyena Milk: His wife will deceive him and be unfaithful to him.

Wolf: It either symbolises a tyrant ruler or a thief who swear false oaths. It may even be the observer's opponent who will swear false oath when he will contest him or have an argument with him.

Drinking Wolf Milk: The one who drinks the milk will attain much goodness in that if he is in grief he will soon find relief and if he is a destitute he will become rich.

Cat: It symbolises a thief.

A Cat Entering a House: If a cat is seen entering a house it means a thief will enter that house. And if it is seen snatching something it means something will be stolen from his house.

Killing a Cat: Killing or slaughtering a cat means that a person will overpower his enemy or rival.

A Cat Fighting Someone: The person with whom the cat is fighting will become ill in the very near future. If the cat is overpowered, he will recover quickly. But if the cat bites him he will remain ill for a lengthy period. According to Imaam Muhammad bin Sireen his illness will span for one whole year. And a wild cat bespeaks of more serious illness and for a greater period.

Mongoose, Lynx or Weasel: The interpretation of any of the above is the same as a cat except that the illness is of a less serious nature and for a shorter period.

An Ape or Monkey: It represents his enemy who is defeated. The reason for his defeat is the fact that Allah has deprived him of his favours because of his sins, infamy and wickedness.

A Swine: It represents a person who has a striking personality but is in fact very wicked in matters of character, conduct and Deen.

Acquiring and Portion of a Swine: Acquiring the meat, blood, hair etc. of a swine means a person will or has acquired unlawful wealth.

Drinking the Milk of a Sow: Drinking such milk means a person will commit evil through his intellect and wealth.

A Dog: A dog symbolises a person's enemy whose enmity hasn't reached its peak and he will soon become his friend. He is also malicious and of mean character and conduct.

A Barking Dog: It symbolises a person of mean character who will utter unpleasant words.

A Dog that Attacks: If a dog is seen attacking and bitting a person it means that the harm caused by his enemy will not be confined to unpleasant words only but bodily harm as well.

A Dog Ripping the Clothes: If a dog is seen attacking and ripping a person's clothes it means that his enemy will humiliate him. The humiliation will be equalled to the extent of the clothes it had ripped.

Eating Dog Meat: Eating dog meat means he will overpower his enemy as well as acquire assets form him.

Training or Holding a Dog: Training or holding a dog so as to safeguard a certain thing means he will be helped by someone in attaining his goal. In this case the dog does not symbolise an enemy.

The Milk of a Bitch: Drinking such milk means he will be afflicted with fright and terror.

Animals with Fangs: They all symbolise one's enemies. The size and strength of such animals is the deciding factor for the strength and power fo such enemies.

And Allah knows best.

Section 20 :

Dreaming of Snakes, Scorpions, and Other Creatures of the Earth

Snakes: A snake symbolises a person's arch enemy. The greater the snake the greater the enemy.

Fighting a Snake: Fighting a snake means a person will fight his enemy. Overpowering it means he will gain victory over him. And if he is overpowered it means he will be defeated.

Being Bitten by a Snake: If a person sees a snake bitting him it means his enemy will harm him as much as he will be harmed by the snake bite.

Killing a Snake: The one who kills the snake will gain victory over his enemy. Leaving the snake in two pieces means he will do likewise to his enemy.

A Snake with Hands and Feet: His enemy is powerful with great resources at this disposal.

Fearing a Snake: Fearing a snake without seeing one means he will be protected against his enemy. He will not be terrorised. And if he sees the snake it means he will be terrorised but no harm will come to him.

A Snake in the House: If a snake is seen entering a person's house then this represents his womenfolk and close relatives who are his enemies. If it is seen leaving his house then they are his distant relatives who are his enemies.

A Snake Leaving a Person's Ear or Stomach: If a snake is seen leaving his ear, stomach or back passage it means he has an enemy amongst his children who will soon part from him.

Possessing a Snake: Possessing a snake in such a manner that he does not feel any fright is suggestive of wielding power and owning vast lands and properties. The greater the snake the greater the lands and properties. Such a snake does not symbolise an enemy.

Possessing a Black Snake: The owner of such a snake will become the leader of an army.

Possessing a Beautiful White Snake: He is a man of good fortune.

Possessing a Smooth and Beautiful Snake: He will acquire fortunes from the treasures of the king.

Scorpion: It symbolises a wicked, cunning and deceitful person who harms a friend and enemy alike. Such a person is very dangerous in that he employs his tongue artfully in causing disharmony amongst people. He has no religion nor is he a man who honours his word.

Getting Stung by a Scorpion: This is an enemy who will speak evil of him.

Killing a Scorpion: He will gain victory over his enemy.

A Scorpion in the Hand: Holding a scorpion in the hand while it stings the people means the person holding the scorpion will speak ill of the people behind their backs.

Eating the Meat of a Scorpion: The person doing so will acquire assets from his enemy.

A Scorpion in the Stomach: A scorpion in the stomach, bed or shirt means a person's enemy is in close proximity with him. He hears all that he says and divulges it to others.

Wasp: It represents an influential but a mean and wicked person. If a swarm of wasps is seen attacking someone it means he will soon become aware of rumours concerning him caused by mean and wicked persons.

Ants: An ant symbolises a zealous and hard working person _ one who toils hard in earning a livelihood and supporting his friends.

Mosquitoes and Butterflies: A mosquito or butterfly represents a mean and contemptuous person.

Bugs: To see a bug in the house means that a person will have a large family.

Bugs Leaving their Nests: The people of that area will emigrate or die.

Locusts: To see locusts in the dream is the same as seeing an army of soldiers in that locality. Havoc and destruction caused by these soldiers will be equal to the havoc and destruction caused by the locusts in the dream. And if soldiers are seen marching in a known area it means locusts will cause destruction in that area.

Black Beetles, Dun-flies and all other types of Flies: They symbolise weak people of little or no standing in society.

Spiders: A spider symbolise a pious person who devotes all his time in worship. He is also a hermit who guards his time and always offers repentance to Allah.

A Story Teller: As opposed to a spider he symbolise a sinful and wicked person for he corrupts the people and incites one against the other.

A Mouse: It represents an evil and wicked woman whether the mouse is a male or female.

Killing a Mouse: He will come in contact or marry an evil and sinful woman.

Incidents Pertaining to this Section

Incident 1: A person related his dream to Imaam Muhammad bin Sireen ﷺ saying that he had seen himself carrying a bag filled with snakes and scorpions. The Imaam interpreted the dream saying that he had done something as to cause the wicked people to hate him. He said: " Yes, I have been appointed by the Sultan to collect taxes from the Arabs. This has caused them to hate me."

Incident 2: Another person revealed his dream to the Imaam saying that he had seen a snake in his house. It had bitten him on the hand and back causing him much pain. The Imaam asked: " You have a brother and a sister?" He said: "Yes." The Imaam said: "Then you have a relative in your home whose heart is filled with malice towards you. Soon he will cause you great harm." The person said: "I have a step brother who has stolen all that I had inherited. He has absconded since three days."

Incident 3: A person said to the learned Imaam that has a glass bowl in which he eats his food. He saw in his dream that it is filled with ants. The Imaam asked him whether he has a wife. He said: "Yes". Then he asked him whether he has a slave as well. He said: "Yes", He said: "Drive him out of your home. There is no goodness in keeping such a slave." The man returned home depressed and worried. When the wife saw him in a depressed state she asked him the reason. He related to him the advice of the Imaam. She asked him what he planned to do. He said he planned to sell him. She said: "In that case you may as well divorce me."

It is said that he sold the slave to a teacher of his. When the wife learned of this she absconded in pursuit of the slave. The husband, on learning this immediately set off to look for her. He found her in the city of Harraan where she had repurchased the slave from his new master and married him.

Section 21 :

Dreaming of Fish and Other Marine Creatures

Fresh Fish: If they are huge and many they symbolise wealth and assets for the one who acquires them. If small and many it means he will be afflicted with grief and sorrow. If one or two, they represent one or two women from who he will derive benefit.

Fillets of Fresh Fish: If the fillets, fat or skin of fresh fish is eaten or acquired by a person it means he will acquire wealth and assets from someone. Perhaps from some authority or woman.

Salted Fish: Salted whether small or big symbolises grief and sorrow caused by a person's servants, subordinates or brother.

Crocodile: It symbolises a thief who is crafty, sly and deceitful. Neither does his enemies nor his friends feel safe with him around.

The Flesh, Skin and Bones of a Crocodile: These symbolise wealth belonging to a person's enemy. Acquiring any of these means he will acquire assets from his enemy.

Frog: If one or two, they symbolise a person who perseveres in offering his devotions to Allah.

Frogs: They represent an army of Allah. Seeing them in an area or house means that the people of such an area or house will soon be visited with the punishment of Allah.

Tortoise or Turtle: It represents a person of great Islamic learning. One who perseveres in acquiring knowledge and acting upon it. He also devotes much of his time in worshipping Allah.

Seeing, owning or bringing one into the house means he will soon build a strong relationship with a man of great learning.

Eating Turtle Meat: He will acquire Islamic knowledge.

A Turtle Walking on the Road: Seeing a turtle walking on the road or in a garbage or in a dumping place means that the inhabitants of that place have little or no regard for Islamic Knowledge. They will soon be deprived of *Ilm* and *Ulama*.

A Turtle in a Protected Environment: Seeing a turtle in a protected environment or sanctuary means that the people of that place appreciate and honour Islamic Knowledge.

Crab: It represent a man of sound character and strong principles. When he makes decisions he does so with confidence. His stoic beliefs sometimes give the impression that he is stern, proud and haughty.

Section 22 :

Seeing Ordinary Birds, Birds of Prey and Poultry in the Dream

Birds of Prey: Generally, birds symbolise sublimity and power enjoyed by kings, monarchs, rulers, governors and chiefs.

Acquiring or Owning a Vulture: If a person dreams that he has acquired or owned a vulture which is trained to obey his commands it means he will acquire assets and estates; he will also wield power by way of his appointment to kingship.

Flying on the Back of a Vulture: If he dreams that he is flying horizontally on the back of a vulture, he will enjoy honour, sublimity and power by being promoted to the office of kingship.

But if the vulture flies with him vertically towards the heavens, he will die while on a journey. For, such a vulture would then represent the angel of death.

Falcon: It symbolises a tyrant ruler or king who is powerful and well known as a warlord. Acquiring or owning a falcon which obeys his commands means he will acquire assets and estates; he will also wield power by way of his appointment to kingship. Similarly, if it is seen flying horizontally with him on its back, he will enjoy honour, sublimity and power by being promoted to the office of kingship. And if it is seen flying with him vertically towards the heavens, he will die while journeying.

The same is the interpretation if he sees a hawk or any other bird of prey.

Kite or Eagle: It symbolises a humble king who maintains a low profile but is extremely powerful.

Owl: It represents a timid and weak thief who has no friends and helpers.

Crow: It represents a mischievous person who is a great liar and an impostor. He has no religion. The same is the interpretation of an old eagle and magpie. Imaam Ibne Sireen ﷺ says that if a person sees and old eagle in his dream during the day, he will suffer from some serious illness.

Wood-pigeon: It symbolises a servant of the king who is well informed on governmental affairs. He advises the king or government in matters relating to national affairs so that the country advances in the right direction. It is also said that he is the financial minister of the state who is experienced, intelligent, farsighted and influential.

Crane: It represents a person from a foreign land who is poor and a destitute.

A Female Ostrich: It represents a bedouin woman.

A Male Ostrich: It represents a man who is a foreigner and unmarried.

A Cock: It represents a man from a foreign land or a slave. It is also said that is represents an announcer such as a mu'azzin.

A Hen: It represents a blessed woman. If many hens are seen then they represent dames and women who will gather together for some happy occasion such as a wedding.

A Partridge or Pheasant: It represents a treacherous and deceitful woman. She has no principles and no good can be expected of her.

A Turtle Dove : A charming lady who loves pleasure and who has a passion for fun and merry-making.

A Parrot: It represents a slave girl or an orphan boy.

Peacock: It symbolises a foreigner in an Arab land; or assets; or beauty and adornment; or a person's followers.

Peahen: It symbolises an attractive and beautiful non-Arab lady. And if the peahen is ugly it symbolises a beautiful woman but not capable of loving or be-loved nor reliable.

A Honey Bee: It symbolises a son who is blessed, dexterous and alert.

A Ring-dove: A ringed turtle dove symbolises an immodest, shameless woman who has no inclination towards Deen.

Eating or Owning a Ring-dove: If a person eats such a dove or owns it, it means he will have some business to do with a woman.

Acquiring the Feathers or Eggs of a Ring-dove: If he acquires its feathers or eggs by trapping it, it means he will coin some deceptive methods of trapping a woman.

Hunting a Ring-dove: Hunting it by any means such as a spear or stone means he will make false accusation against a woman.

Nightingale: It represents a blessed baby boy or a loyal servant or slave.

A Crested Bird: It represents a small child.

Sparrow: A male sparrow symbolises an obese dangerous person. A female symbolises a cursed woman.

Hunting Sparrows: A great many sparrows symbolise assets, wealth and booty provided they are hunted.

The Chirping of Birds: A glad tiding will be received.

A Flock of Small Birds (*Ababeel*): Such a flock symbolises a blessed person who devotes his time in worshipping Allah profusely.

Starling: It represents a person who constantly undertakes journeys.

Raven: Seeing this bird means he will be guided on the straight path.

Marine Birds: They symbolise the ministers of the king or government or their officers and official if such birds are seen in the water. But if they are seen on dry land it means prosperity, freshness and verdure. And if the birds are green it means grief, sorrow and perplexity.

Birds of Unknown Species: They symbolise the angels. Their interpretation is the same as that of seeing the angels of Allah Ta'ala.

Eggs of Unknown Birds: They represent beautiful women with handsome faces if the beholder of the dream becomes the owner of the eggs or he finds them in his possession.

Eating the Eggs of Unknown Birds: The one who eats them cooked, fried or boiled in his dream, will acquire riches and prosperity.

Eating Uncooked Eggs: He will receive *haraam* wealth.

Eating the Shell or White of the Egg: Eating the shell or white of the egg but not the yolk means he will usurp wealth belonging to the deceased or a slain person. It could also mean that he will dig up graves for the purpose of stealing the shroud (*kafn*) of the dead people.

And Allah knows best.

Incidents Relating to this Section

Incident 1: A person related his dream to Imaam Muhammad bin Sireen رحمة الله, saying that he had seen a white pigeon sitting on the pinnacle of a masjid in Madinah and that he was captivated by its beauty. Then came a hawk and carried it way. The Imaam said: "If you are speaking the truth it means Hajjaj bin Yoosuf will marry the daughter of Abdullah bin Ja'far At-Tayyaar."

It is said that not many days had passed before Hajjaj married her. Someone asked Ibne Sireen: "O Abu Abdullah, how did you happen to come to this interpretation?" He replied: "A pigeon symbolise a woman. It s whiteness represents her beauty. The pinnacle of the masjid bespeaks her nobility and honour. And I found no other woman with such beauty and honour except the daughter of At-Tayyar. Then I looked at the hawk which symbolises a tyrant and despotic ruler. I found Hajjaj fitting this description. This is how I reached this interpretation." It is said that all the people sitting in his *majlis* were awe-struck when they heard this explanation of his.

Incident 2: Another person related the following dream to the Imaam: He had seen a fat bird of an unknown species descending from the sky and sitting on a tree. It started packing at the blossoms of the tree and thereafter flew away. At this juncture, the Imaam's face turned pale. He said: "This is an indication of some great men of learning passing away." It is said that Hasan Al-Basri and Ibne Sireen passed away that very year.

Incident 3: It is related the Umar bin Al-Khattaab ﷺ saw that a cock packed at him once or twice. Someone asked him what the dream meant. He said: "A non-Arab person will kill me soon." It is said that within four days of the dream Aboo Lulu killed him. May Allah be pleased with him.

Incident 4: A person asked Imaam Muhammad bin Sireen ﷺ "What is your opinion regarding a person who had dreamed that he broke an egg and ate its white only and not its yolk?" The Imaam said: "Bring me the man who had seen the dream so that her personally relates to me his dream. I will answer him." The man said: "No, do answer me: I will convey your interpretation to him." The Imaam refused. He insisted several times and the Imaam refused the same number of times. Finally he said under oath: "My Lord, by Allah, it is I who had seen the dream." The Imaam said to the people around him: "Catch him and hand him over to the authorities, for he digs up graves and steals the *kafn* from the dead!"He pleaded: "My Lord, I sincerely repent to Allah before you! I promise never to commit this sin again all my life!" Thus, he was not handed over to the authorities, but was released.

Incident 5: It is related that a person revealed his dream to the Imaam saying that he had seen himself holding a water-bird, trying to slaughter it with a knife thrice. Each time the bird managed to struggle itself loose. The fourth time he succeeded. To this the Imaam said: "You have seen a good dream. This is a virgin woman whom you wished to bring under your control thrice but without success. You succeeded the fourth time." He said: "My Lord, you have spoken the truth. Tonight will be the near me. Once more thing remains to be told." The man drew closer and asked: "What remains to be told, my Lord?" He said: "The girl let loose wind aloud as well." He said: "Yes, you have spoken the truth." He felt ashamed and departed.

Allah knows best.

Section 23 :

Dreaming of Professionals, Manufacturers, Tradesmen, Entertainers etc.

A Person Who Weighs and Measures: He symbolises a qaadhi, judge or magistrate if he is unknown. If a person sees such a person clapping hands it means the *qaadhi* is biased and unfair in his judgement. And if he is seen dancing he is fair and impartial.

If a person sees himself taking up the trade of weighing or measuring it means he will be appointed as a judge.

An Unknown *Qaadhi* **or Judge:** It is non other than Allah Ta'ala.

A Khateeb: He symbolises a *faqeeh*, jurist and a man of great Islamic learning.

Perfumer: As above, he symbolises a *faqeeh*, jurist and a man of great Islamic learning.

Money-changer: He symbolises an *aalim* from whom people derive no benefit except material benefit.

Cloth Merchant: He symbolises a man of high standing in the community; or he symbolises a poet or a man of wisdom.

Treasurer: A great poet who is artful in humiliating people through his poetry.

Tailor: A man who his religion for the material things of this world; or a man who is indispensable in the worldly affairs of people.

Dealer in Hide and Skin: A wealthy man who earns his wealth through pure and lawful means.

One who Mends s Patches: A man who loves to quarrel.

Cobbler: A man who joins people's hearts. He is very influential in forging unity between husbands and wives.

Slave Trader: One who is well acquainted with matters relating to the king or government.

Carpenter: A man who subdues people. He has great influential powers.

Blacksmith: A person who owns vast estates, exercises control and wields power.

A Wine Merchant: He pursues whatever comes his way, good or bad.

Launderer: He symbolises a person who dislikes people for the evil they do. He urges them to offer sincere repentance.

Chef or Cook: A person who talks incessantly in order to acquire his livelihood. He also acquires much good.

Butcher: If he is unknown he symbolises the angel of death. If known it is a person who is ever on the run to acquire riches.

Sailor or Navigator: He symbolises a person who knows how to cure people of their sicknesses whether they are rulers or subjects.

Goldsmith: A compulsive liar. He deceives people. He is a mean fellow because of his doings.

Phlebotomist: He symbolises a writer or an author.

Writer: He symbolises a phlebotomist ★.

Cotton-carder: A truthful, honest and upright person who is able to distinguish right from wrong, truth from falsehood, good from bad.

★ Phlebotomy is the act of bloodletting as a means of therapeutic measure _ Collins Concise Eng. Dic.

Miller: He represents a porter or one who hires out animals.

Cup-bearer★: One who has many friends, relatives and acquaintances.

Saddler: A man who causes a rift between a man and his wife.

Dyer: One who is deceitful, pretentious and a compulsive liar. He loves to show off and be boastful. He makes false allegations against people.

Greengrocer: A person who fully comprehends what people say and he understands their reasoning. And when he speaks he supports his speech with good reasoning and proof. He also possesses a good and clean heart.

Minter: He symbolises a person who causes disturbance, disunity and ill feelings in the community. He rouses people against one another.

Barber: He symbolises a wealth person who is an asset to the community yet has the ability to cause it great harm.

Shield Maker: A person who transports people from one place to another.

Basket Maker: A wealthy person who can cause benefit or harm. The same is the interpretation of seeing a slaughterer, glass manufacturer, fuller and diver.

Teacher, Ustaad, Tutor etc.: Represents a friend or a king or his minister. And if a person sees himself sitting with the pupils or students in the *madrasah* it means he will live long and reach a good old age.

Weaver: A traveller.

Treasure Collector: A person who has a huge family but is barely able to support his family.

★ A cup-bearer is a person who fills and serves the wine cups, as in a king's palace _ Collins Concise Eng. Dic.

Builder: A person at whose hands people offer repentance and swear oaths of abstinence from sins.

Surgeon: Represents a liar or a con man or a person who exercise *sihr* or *jaadoo*.

Astrologer, Soothsayer, Magician etc.: Any of the above symbolises a great liar who may also be very close to the king or government.

One who Makes Ta'weez: He represents a person who is master at the art of convincing people by the sweetness of his tongue.

Conjurer or *Raaqi*: Persons who makes *dam* on people represent government officials.

Fishmonger: He symbolises a leader or chief in the community.

Painter: One who invents a lie against Allah.

Shroud-thief: If seen by a trustworthy person who advocates peace and harmony it means he will acquire tremendous knowledge and wisdom. But if he is not trustworthy and does not advocate peace and harmony it means he will pursue the material things of this world.

Grave Digger and Excavator: To see a grave digger or excavator in the dream means death for the one who sees it provided any of the following happens: He pushes the grave digger away from his place; his animal tramples the grave digger; the grave digger falls on the ground; he himself is in the state of *sakraat*. But if any of the following happens then he will either lose his job or die: he rolls up his bedding; his turban or *topi* falls off from his head; his hand gets cut off from his body; his tongue is cut off; he becomes blind.

And Allah knows best.

Section 24 :

Miscellaneous

Noor and Darkness: *Noor* means *hidaayat* (guidance) while darkness means deviation and misleading others.

Ruins and Desolate Land: Ruins and land that is laid waste means going astray and misleading others.

Fort: Protection and security for the one who enters it.

Books and Magazines: Books and magazines that are rolled up in a bundle symbolise news that is concealed. Books that are laid open symbolise news that is plain and obvious.

Seal: The matter is under probation.

Sealed Books: It means riches and fortunes a person will inherit, for Allah said to Yahya ﷺ: *O Yahya, hold on to the book with strength* when he was to inherit the Torah from Zakariyya ﷺ.

Books of Hadeeth and Fiqh: Books of Hadeeth and Fiqh symbolise knowledge and wisdom. Books of poetry mean deviation, deception and falsehood.

The Holy Qur'aan: Seeing the Holy Qur'aan in the dream means a person will acquire knowledge and wisdom. And writing it means he will acquire Deen, knowledge, wisdom and material wealth through which he will help others.

Desecrating the Holy Qur'aan: Tearing or destroying the Holy Qur'aan means he is guilty of negating the Holy Qur'aan. Eating its pages means he is making fun of it; he has no regard for its laws; he treats it with contempt.

Limbs of the Body becoming Iron: If a person sees his arms, calves of the legs, clothes etc. becoming iron it means her will attain a long life.

Becoming a Slave or Prisoner: He will soon find himself in a desperate situation by losing his wealth and respect. He will be afflicted with grief and sorrow.

Limbs of The Body Becoming Glass: If any of the limbs becomes glass, the person has a very short life span.

Lending or Borrowing Something: It symbolises his profits and gains which will remain in safe custody.

Buying or Selling a Slave: Selling a slave means he will find relief from his grief and sorrows. Buying him means he will be afflicted with grief and sorrow. It is said that buying a slave girl is better than selling her.

Musk: Seeing musk in the dream is an indication of joy and happiness

Oud: Smelling or burning *oud* means people will speak well of him. The same applies to all fragrant incenses such as *agarbatti, loban* etc.

Saffron: Accumulated wealth that is pure and *halaal*. If a person dyes something using saffron, he will fall ill.

Usfar: Its interpretation is the same as saffron. *Usfar* is a red flower used for dyeing clothes.

Frankincense: It symbolises the correct understanding of Deen which a person will acquire from some auspicious and blessed person.

Honey: It represents a person's accumulated wealth. At times it is wealth that he has inherited or will inherit. It also symbolises Islamic and Qur'aanic knowledge.

Any sweetmeats mad of honey or sugar symbolises a person's wealth and *halaal rizq*.

Preparing Sweetmeats: If a person prepares it with his own hands it means increment in his *rizq*. But if someone else prepares it, it represents wealth he will inherit.

Marriage: Cure from all diseases and ailments.

Sugar: Sugar as well as sweetness represent money and riches if a person eats it. Sometimes it means sweet utterances.

Medicines: Taking or using medicine means cure from sickness, protection against all ailments and the acquiring of good health and blessedness.

Eid: Witnessing any of the two Islamic festivals in the dream means an end to all his perplexities, grief and sorrow. It also means increase in his *rizq*.

Mourning: Mourning means rejoicing and rejoicing means mourning.

Merry Making: Merry making means grief and grief means merry making.

Restriction: It symbolises firmness and steadfastness. And restrictions are of various types:

Restriction in the Masjid: Restriction in the masjid or in the act of salah or in the path of Allah means the person will be firm in matters of Deen and he will abstain from committing sins.

Restriction in a City, House or Village: He will marry soon.

In Chains: If a person dreams that his legs are chained or tied with something or they are entangled in a net or they are stuck in a hole or well it means he will continue deceiving, cheating and robbing people.

Saddling a Horse: He will meet up with some woman.

Chess: False utterances, lies and allegations. Also arguments.

Dice: News that cannot be confirmed nor supported by evidence.

Chessman: Any chessman other than a pawn symbolises disturbance, tumult and argument. The same is the interpretation if a person uses walnuts or almonds instead of chessman in a chess game.

Ink Pot or Ink Bottle: It symbolises a woman. If it breaks or is stolen his wife will die.

Pen, Pencil etc.: If a pen is seen with the Holy Qur'an it symbolises knowledge and wisdom; if seen with an ink pot it is a son.

Desires fulfilled: If a person dreams that his mission is accomplished and his heart's desires are fulfilled in the world it means his condition will change completely and he will sustain much loss for Allah Ta'ala says in the Holy Qur'aan: *Until in the midst of their enjoyment of our gifts, We called them to account suddenly, when lo, they were plunged in despair.*

Likewise, a poet has said: When the mission is accomplished loss becomes apparent; wait for fall and decline as soon as it is said finished!

Note: It should be noted that when relating a dream it should be done without adding anything to it or subtracting anything from it. For, if a person does this he spoils and corrupts the dream. Moreover, Rasoolullah ﷺ has strongly prohibited anyone from doing this.

He is reported as saying that anyone who invents a lie linking it to him (ie. Rasoolullah ﷺ let him make his abode in hell-fire.

He is also reported as saying that anyone who invents a lie linking it to him or his (own) father or friend, he will not even smell the sweet fragrance of Jannah.

He is also reported as saying: "There are three persons whom Allah will punish severely on the Day of Qiyaamah: a person who relates a false dream: he will be made to tie a knot between two grains of barley which he will never be able to do; a man who paints a picture of animate objects: he will be made to put life into them which he will never be able to do; a man leads a people in Salaah while they dislike him."

It is advisable for a person who sees an unpleasant or disturbing dream that he spits thrice on his left side as soon as he awakes up and thereafter seek Allah's protection from the accursed devil. Rasoolullah ﷺ and his followers used to do likewise.

Section 25 :

Reciting the Various *Suwar* of the Holy Qur'aan in the Dream

Soorah Faatihah: Anyone who recites it fully or partially, his duas will be assuredly accepted by Allah and he will derive such benefit thereby that it will bring him joy and happiness. Some say that he will marry seven women in succession and his duas will be accepted. This is borne out by the fact that Rasoolullah ﷺ used to recite *Alhamdu lillahi rabbil aalameen* in the beginning of his dua as well as at the end.

Soorah Baqarah: whoever reads it in his dream fully or partially _ albeit one word _ he will live long and progress in deeds of piety. At times it means he will move to a new locality where he will be revered and honoured. Some say that if he is a *qaadhi* (judge) his departure from this world is imminent and if he an *aalim* his life span will be long and his condition will improve.

Soorah Aale Imraan: Whoever reads it in his dream fully or partially he will be the black sheep of his family. He will acquire his *rizq* in old age. He will also undertake journeys continuously.

Soorah Nisaa: The reader will live with a beautiful woman till the end of his life. But the marriage will not be a happy one. He will also possess the ability to present strong arguments and speak eloquently.

Soorah Maa'idah: The reader of this Soorah will be a noble person whose passion will be to feed people. But at length he will be harmed by some hard-hearted persons.

Soorah An'aam: Its reader will now focus his attention towards safeguarding and serving the cause of Seen. He will acquire *halaal rizq* and will be fortunate in the world and hereafter.

Soorah A'raaf: Its reader will acquire a little knowledge of every sicence. And it is possible that he will die in a foreign land.

Soorah Anfaal: Its reader will be crowned with honour and his Deen will remain safeguarded.

Soorah Taubah: Whoever reads it in his dream, he will revere and love the pious people.

Soorah Yoonus: Its reader will suffer some loss of wealth. It is also said that its reader will become a bearer of glad tidings at all times.

Soorah Hood: He will have lots of enemies and will choose to live in a foreign land rather than his own.

Soorah Yoosuf: Whoever reads it in his dream his family members will become his enemies and his livelihood will be received in a land away from home.

Soorah Ra'ad: Its reader will always be impoverished and needy. According to one interpretation his death is imminent.

Soorah Ibraheem: Its reader will glorify Allah abundantly and he will offer abundant repentance unto Allah.

Soorah Hijr: Whoever reads it in his dream his family will be protected against all calamities and he will become humble and submissive. And if its reader is a king his death is imminent. If he is a *qaadhi* his conduct and character will be good. If a trader he will enjoy certain privileges over his family. If an *aalim* he will die an honourable death.

Soorah Nahl: The one who reads it in his dream, his *rizq* will be safeguarded. He will be included amongst the party of the beloved Prophet ﷺ even though he did not witness his company.

Soorah Bani Isra'eel: The king or government will subject its reader to tyranny and oppression. It is also said that he will be safeguarded against the mischief of certain persons while fearing a crisis of which he will be innocent.

Soorah Kahf: Its reader will be blessed with a long life, he will live under pleasant circumstances, his condition will improve and he will receive sustenance from the people who give him shelter and protection.

Soorah Maryam: Whoever reads this Soorah in his dream he will find himself in straitened circumstances but Allah will remove his difficulties and ease matters for him.

Soorah Taha: Whoever reads it will love performing the *tahajjud salaah* and do good deeds. Moreover, he will spend his time in the company of pious people.

Soorah Ambiya: Its reader will think well of the people.

Soorah Hajj: He will perform Hajj and Umrah. But if he is ill he will die.

Soorah Mu'minoon: Reading it is an indication that he loves offering long prayers and displaying his submission to Allah during the nights. But there is fear that he will be afflicted with some serious illness.

Soorah Noor: Its reader will be amongst those who enjoin what is right and forbid what is wrong; he will love some and dislike others for the sake of Allah; he will be afflicted with some illness.

Soorah Furqaan: He will love truth and abhor falsehood.

Soorah Shu'ara: He will earn his livelihood with much hardship. He will not acquire anything but with difficulties. He will take to long journeys but achieve very little.

Soorah Naml: He will truth and abhor falsehood. He will be the leader of his people. He will acquire knowledge and power.

Soorah Qasas: Whoever recites this Soorah he will be tested in the matter of a piece of land. This piece of land may be in the countryside, city, his home or in the place where he performs his salaah.

Soorah Ankaboot: Its reader is given the glad tiding from Allah that he will not be put to test.

Soorah Room: Whoever reads it there is hypocrisy in his heart. But if its reader is a king he will acquire the knowledge of Deen. And if he a *qaadhi* or trader he will profit tremendously.

Soorah Luqmaan: whoever reads it he will become a good calligrapher and acquire wisdom.

Soorah Sajdah: Its reader will become a firm *mu-wahhid* (Unitarian) and a strong believer.

Soorah Ahzaab: Its reader will praise his family members; he will be granted longevity; and he will be very cunning to is friends.

Soorah Sabaa: The one who recites this Soorah will become brave and ever eager to arm himself with a sword.

Soorah Faatir: Its reciter will see Allah Ta'ala and become a saint from amongst the saints of Allah.

Soorah Yaseen: He will remain steadfast on his Deen.

Soorah Saaffaat: He will receive his livelihood from *halaal* sources and be blessed with two male offsprings.

Soorah Saad: Its reader will have much sense of honour. He will also display much love for women, familiarising and travelling with them.

Soorah Zumar: Its reader will live long enough to see his grand children. Perhaps he will travel to some palace never to return.

Soorah Mu'min or Ghaafir: He will be a firm believer.

Soorah Ha-Meem As-Sajdah: Its reader will become a means of *hidaayat* and guidance for the people.

Soorah Shoora : Its reader will benefit from his *ilm* and *amal*.

Soorah Zukhruf: The one who recites it in his dream will acquire his livelihood with much difficulty and he will be less fortunate during the final years of his life.

Soorah Dukhaan: The one recites it in his dream will be safeguarded against harms caused by oppressors; he will also be granted protection from the chastisement of the grave and punishment of hell-fire. He will not weaken in his beliefs.

Soorah Jaathiyah: Its reader will lead an ascetic life (ie. he will become a *zaahid*).

Soorah Ahqaaf: Its reader will become disobedient to his parents but will repent for his sin during the last stages of his life.

Soorah Muhammad or Qitaal: He will be visited by an angel in its best and most pleasant form.

Soorah Fat-h: Its reader will be loved by Allah.

Soorah Hujuraat: Its reader will become instrumental in joining the hearts of Allah's servants.

Soorah Qaaf: He will acquire knowledge through which people will become obligated to him. The latter part of his life will be better than the former and he will remain steadfast and firm.

Soorah Thaariyaat: Its reader will be able to acquire as much produce of the earth as he desires. And if could also mean that he will live in harmony with people of all religions and *mathaahib*.

Soorah Toor: The one who reads it, Allah will be pleased regarding the matters of his religion.

Soorah Najm: Whoever reads it will be blessed with many children who will die for the pleasure of Allah Ta'ala. Also he will be a man of great learning ane piety.

Soorah Qamar: Sorcery (*jaadu*) will be exercised on its reader but he will not be harmed by the grace of Allah.

Soorah Rahmaan: Its reader will be bestowed with the bounties of Allah in the world and His mercies in the hereafter.

Soorah Waaqi'ah: Its reader will hasten towards performing good deeds and obeying Allah.

Soorah Hadeed: Its reader will accomplish works that will leave lasting impressions on the people. He will also tread the right path and adopt the correct Deen.

Soorah Mujaadalah: Its reader will fight against those who profess falsehood and he will be stern with them.

Soorah Hashr: He will be resurrected while Allah will be pleased with him; he will also destroy his enemies.

Soorah Mumtahinah: Its reader will find himself in some difficulty while he will be rewarded for it.

Soorah Saff: Its reader will die as a martyr.

Soorah Jumu'ah: Allah will gather for him the bounties of both the worlds.

Soorah Munafiqoon: Its reader will be exonerated from *nifaaq* and hypocrisy.

Soorah Taghaabun: He will die on *hidaayah* and guidance.

Soorah Talaaq: Its reader will have disputes with his wife which will lead to a divorce. But he will pay in full her dowry.

Soorah Tahreem: He will abstain from violating the laws of Allah regarding *haraam*.

Soorah Mulk: Allah will grant him the bounties of both the worlds. He will own a great deal of properties and give much charity.

Soorah Noon or Qalam: Allah will shower His blessings on him and he will attain salvation.

Soorah Haaqqah: There is fear that its reader will become subjected to some aggression although he will be on the right.

Soorah Ma'aarij: Its reader will be protected and helped by

Allah. He will be successful.

Soorah Nooh: Whoever reads it in his dream will be amongst those who enjoin what is right and forbid what is wrong. He will also be helped against his enemies.

Soorah Jinn: Its reader will be protected against jinn.

Soorah Muzzammil: Its reciter will be a man of good conduct and he will exercise patience and *sabr* and always be grateful to Allah.

Soorah Muddath-thir: The one who reads it will be in straitened circumstances but Allah will remove his difficulties.

Soorah Qiyaamah: Its reader will always abstain from swearing oaths.

Soorah Dahr or Insaan: Its reader will be a generous man who will also be grateful to Allah for His bounties.

Soorah Mursalaat: Allah will increase his *rizq* for him and guide him to be grateful to Him at all times.

Soorah Naba': All grief and sorrow will be removed form his heart. He will become honourable and his name will be mentioned with reverence by the people.

Soorah Naazi'aat: Its reader will discharge his zakaah and give much charity.

Soorah Abasa: Its reader will discharge his zakaah and give much charity.

Soorah Takweer: Its reader will travel a great deal to the East and his journeys will prove fruitful.

Soorah Infitaar: The kings and rulers will hold him dear and they will honour him.

Soorah Tatfeef: He will be guided to become faithful and just.

Soorah Inshiqaaq: He will have many offsprings.

Soorah Burooj: Allah will remove his grief and bestow him with honour by granting him knowledge in a variety of Islamic sciences.

Soorah Taariq: Allah will grant him the fervour to remember and glorify Him abundantly.

Soorah A'la: Allah will ease his matters for him.

Soorah Ghaashiyah: He will become esteemed in the eyes of people and the effects of his knowledge will spread far and wide.

Soorah Fajr: He will instil awe and elegance in the hearts of people.

Soorah Balad: Its reader will feed the poor, love the orphans and show kindness to the weak.

Soorah Shams: Allah will grant its reader intellect and farsightedness in all matters.

Soorah Layl: Allah will grant its reader protection against humiliation.

Soorah Duhaa: Its reader will honour the orphans and indigent people.

Soorah Inshiraah: Allah will open his bosom so that he acquires the correct understanding of Deen. Allah will also ease matters for him and remove his sorrow.

Soorah Teen: Allah will hastily fulfil his needs and grant him sustenance without any difficulty.

Soorah Alaq: He will be granted longevity and his status will be raised.

Soorah Qadr: It recitation is an indication that he will do good actions.

Soorah Bayyinah: Allah will make him a means of guidance for pious people.

Soorah Zilzaal: Allah will grant him the power and strength to weaken the non-believers.

Soorah Aadiyaat: Allah will grant him horses of such qualities that he will be able to derive much benefit from them.

Soorah Qaari'ah: Allah will grant him honour through worship and *taqwa*.

Soorah Takaathur or Maqaabir: Its reader will stop amassing wealth and lead and ascetic life.

Soorah Asr: Its reader will exercise *sabr* and patience and he will help in matters of truth.

Soorah Humazah: Its reader will amass wealth and then spend it in good causes.

Soorah Feel: He will be helped against the enemy and Islam will become victorious at his hands.

Soorah Quraish: Its reader will feed the poor and Allah will make him the means of joining the hearts of the Muslims.

Soorah Maa'oon: Its reader will gain victory over his opposition.

Soorah Kauthar: Its reader will acquire much goodness in both the worlds.

Soorah Kaafiroon: Its reader will fight against the non-believers.

Soorah Nasr: Allah will help it reader against his enemies. Perhaps its recitation is an indication of his death in the near future. For, it was specifically revealed to Rasoolullah صلى الله عليه وسلم to inform him about his death.

A person said to Ibne Sireen رحمة الله عليه that he had dreamed as if he were reciting Soorah Nasr. He said to him: "Make out your will. Your time has drawn near." He asked: "Why?" He replied: "Because it was the last Soorah revealed to Rasoolullah صلى الله عليه وسلم."

Soorah Lahab or Masad: Whoever recites it in his dream his ambitions will be fulfilled, people will mention his name with reverence, he will become firm in his beliefs, his family will be small and his life will pass with ease and comfort.

Soorah Ikhlaas: Whoever reads it will repent for his sins and no child of his will live, for Allah says: *He does not beget nor is he begotten.*

Some Ulama say that its recitation in the dream is an indication that the reader will be a *muwahhid* (ie monotheist). Moreover, he will have a son who will live so long that he will be the last amongst his family members to die.

Soorah Falaq: Its reader will be protected against evil.

Soorah Naas: It s reader will be safeguarded against all calamities and granted refuge from the accursed devil.

This is the termination of all that was related from Imaam Muhammad bin Sireen .

❀❀❀

Translation completed on 12 Zil-Hijjah 1413/2 June 1993 at Lenasia _ by the grace and mercy of Allah, The All Powerful, The All Merciful. *Alhamdulillah.* (Translator)